Evangelism Where You Live

Engaging
Your
Community

Stephen Pate and Gene Wilkes

CHALICE
PRESS

ST. LOUIS, MISSOURI

All Scripture, unless otherwise marked, is taken from the *NEW AMERICAN STANDARD BIBLE* ®, © Copyright The Lockman Foundation 1960, 1962, 1963, 1968, 1971, 1972, 1973, 1975, 1977, 1995. Used by permission.

Scripture quotations marked (NIV) are taken from the HOLY BIBLE, NEW INTERNATIONAL VERSION®. NIV®. Copyright © 1973, 1978, 1984 by International Bible Society. Used by permission of Zondervan Publishing House. All rights reserved.

Cover image: FotoSearch

Cover and interior design: Elizabeth Wright

Visit Chalice Press on the World Wide Web at
www.chalicepress.com

10 9 8 7 6 5 4 3 2 1   08   09   10   11   12   13

Library of Congress Cataloging-in-Publication Data

Pate, Steve A., 1953-

Evangelism where you live : engaging your community / by Stephen Pate and C.
Gene Wilkes.

p. cm.

ISBN 978-0-8272-0822-3

1. Evangelistic work. I. Wilkes, C. Gene. II. Title.

BV3790.P33 2008

269'.2--dc22

2008023013

Printed in the United States of America

Contents

**The Columbia Partnership Leadership Series
from Chalice Press**

www.chalicepress.com
www.thecolumbiapartnership.org

Editor's Foreword

Inspiration and Wisdom for Twenty-First–Century Christian Leaders

You have chosen wisely in deciding to study and learn from a book published in **The Columbia Partnership Leadership Series** with Chalice Press. We publish for

- Congregational leaders who desire to serve with greater faithfulness, effectiveness, and innovation.
- Christian ministers who seek to pursue and sustain excellence in ministry service.
- Members of congregations who desire to reach their full kingdom potential.
- Christian leaders who desire to use a coach approach in their ministry.
- Denominational and parachurch leaders who want to come alongside affiliated congregations in a servant leadership role.
- Consultants and coaches who desire to increase their learning concerning the congregations and Christian leaders they serve.

The Columbia Partnership Leadership Series is an inspiration- and wisdom-sharing vehicle of The Columbia Partnership, a community of Christian leaders who are seeking to transform the capacity of the North American Protestant church to pursue and sustain vital Christ-centered ministry. You can connect with us at www.TheColumbiaPartnership.org.

Primarily serving congregations, denominations, educational institutions, leadership development programs, and parachurch organizations, the Partnership also seeks to connect with individuals, businesses, and other organizations seeking a Christ-centered spiritual focus.

We welcome your comments on these books, and we welcome your suggestions for new subject areas and authors we ought to consider.

George W. Bullard Jr., Senior Editor
GBullard@TheColumbiaPartnership.org

The Columbia Partnership,
332 Valley Springs Road, Columbia, SC 29223-6934
Voice: 803.622.0923, www.TheColumbiaPartnership.org

A Tribute to Ron S. Lewis

Life in full-time ministry is a roller-coaster ride. When things are going right, there is nothing like it. But when the pressures, conflicts, broken relationships, and the frustrations of not living up to the expectations we place on ourselves squeeze us, ministry can take us down faster than we can imagine. To find an individual that is readily available to provide wise counsel as a mentor and friend in such times is a genuine gift from God.

Ron S. Lewis was that mentor and friend for both of us. I (Steve) first met Ron in the late 1970s while he was leading his own company, Church Growth Design, out of Nashville, Tennessee. He immediately had my attention. A passion to see people come into a personal relationship with Christ drove his emotions and actions. He flat out loved Jesus and wanted everyone to know Him. He lived a life demonstrating the fact that "all men and women everywhere need God. As Christians, our job is to make that search easy." Both of us fondly remember our monthly lunches with Ron while he later served as senior pastor of the Heights Church in Richardson, Texas, before he returned again to serve churches through Church Growth Design.

Ron continued to read, study, observe, and provide direction to many pastors and churches across the U.S. until cancer took him from us far too early in 2006. We still marvel at the fact that Ron became a proponent of the small group movement and emergent missional churches before both were recognized as "cool." Many of the twenty- and thirty-something pastors leading churches today would consider him engaged and aware of these movements. Our joy is that we can share some of his insights and passion with you in the never-before-published items we share in this book.

Introduction

Bruce is a Canadian who loves hockey but lives and works in Texas. He is also a Christ-follower and a member of the church leadership team at Legacy Church, where Gene is the senior pastor. Bruce began to coach a local hockey team as his son and daughter rose through the skill levels and developed increasing enthusiasm about the sport, but he soon discovered that more and more practices and games fell on Sunday mornings. One day Bruce came to the leadership team and asked that they begin to pray with him about how he should balance his church leadership with coaching the team and their families. He wanted to lead by example to those who were part of Legacy Church by being there when they gathered for worship and for LifeGroups, but he also felt called to coach this team.

One way we describe how we do church at Legacy is that we are "a mission outpost where every member is a missionary in his or her own mission field." To follow Christ means living out your faith wherever God has planted you and wherever your passions and skills lead you to a network of people where you are a missionary of Christ's love, where maybe no one else would tell the gospel. The leadership team unanimously agreed that Bruce did not need to worry about missing an occasional Sunday morning, but that as he led the hockey team he would model the mission of the church. We said that we would rather he model our mission than attend 100 percent of the worship services on Sunday mornings.

A few months into his coaching efforts, Bruce came back to the leadership team to ask that we begin to pray with him about starting a chapel time for the team before practices and games scheduled on Sunday mornings. He had never done anything like this before. He said the chapels would be voluntary in attendance, with a time of scripture study and prayer, and he hoped not only to provide spiritual instruction for those who knew Jesus but also to be a witness to those who did not. Bruce initially thought that he would provide hockey chapels to "those families that would normally find themselves in church." To his amazement Bruce found more than half the families that attended the hockey chapels were unchurched. It appeared that the hockey chapel might be the closest thing to church some of these families would ever see. All but a few team members and their families accepted the concept, and Bruce continued to live out his calling as

1

a Christ-follower in the rink of his passion. He would tell us about the chapels when we had times of prayer as a leadership team, and we celebrated what God was doing through him and for the families who participated in them.

Not everyone was as enthusiastic about the chapel as Bruce and the Christian families on the team. One family of another faith challenged him directly about offering chapel in the rink where the team practiced or played. The proximity of the meeting seemed like undue pressure on those who did not want to attend. After an open discussion with the family, they worked out a compromise to hold the chapels in either a restaurant or food court next to the rinks. The family was satisfied, and the chapels continued.

In the off-season of 2006, Bruce attended a hockey coaches' clinic in Canada. There he "happened" to meet another coach who was the director of a ministry that provided hockey chapels for professional and semi-professional leagues in North America. As they talked, his newfound friend mentioned he had heard about a youth hockey coach in Texas who had begun hockey chapels with his team. Bruce smiled and said, "That's me." Coincidence? We don't think so. The two coaches committed to remain networked to expand the chapel concept to other youth hockey teams and tournaments in the Dallas area.

In the summer of 2007, Bruce came to a church leadership team meeting on a Sunday afternoon. He said that his son and a few of his players from his team attended a Hockey Ministries International weeklong camp that his Canadian contact directed. He began to show emotion as he continued his story, "When I arrived at the end of the camp to pick up my son, the dad of one of my players came over and told me that his son rushed up to him as soon as he saw him and said, 'Dad, guess what. I trusted Jesus as my Savior.'" Bruce paused. He then said, "His father said, 'Bruce, I have you to thank for that.'" We were silent as Bruce tried to hold back his tears. He then said in broken phrases, "I thought I always had to be in church on Sunday mornings, but you guys encouraged me to join my passion for hockey with my love for Christ." He didn't finish his thought, but we knew one of his players was in the family of God because he had followed Jesus into the mission field of hockey in his hometown. We celebrated the fact that God used Bruce's passion and mission, combined, to rescue this young life from the dominion of darkness (Col. 1:13).

Bruce's story is the story of what this book is about. Community-Based Servant Evangelism (CBSE) is a way of doing ministry in which Christ-followers model, encourage, and equip others to be salt and light servants where they live. It is not about church attendance and Bible study, or another program of evangelism. CBSE is about living out the Great Commandment and the Great Commission in our network of relationships in the marketplace and neighborhoods. It is the church on mission, not the church in maintenance. It is Christ-followers who live like salt and light servants to address the needs of their community in the name of Jesus.

We believe Christ is leading His church, or, *ekklesia,* outside the walls it has erected for itself, back into the marketplace and neighborhoods where it began and flourished. The ekklesia is at its best when it is on mission and it's members are organically part of its cultural context, being salt and light servants to those with whom they share life. We find ourselves in what some are calling the "missional movement," which is characterized by writers like Allan Roxburgh,[1] Eddie Gibbs, and Ryan Bolger.[2] Christ is calling again the "called-out ones," who are the *ekklesia tou Christou,* Christ's church. Christ wants them to become servants to their co-mission with Christ. As they go about their lives, they are to love and serve those around them, as Jesus did, so that their friends, business associates, and acquaintances too may call Him their Leader and Rescuer. We believe Christ's call to His followers to live out the Great Commandment and Great Commission is how we are to be and do the work as the ekklesia in the world.

Chapter 1 lays the foundation for this philosophy of ministry. We will assess why our current methods of evangelism are ineffective and propose how CBSE is consistent with Christ's commands to "love God and love others" and to "make disciples of all people." In chapter 2 we will delineate the barriers that churches have built that keep them within the walls of their buildings and out of the mission field Christ has called them to enter.

Chapter 3 describes the concept of "Place" and its importance for grasping both the issue of volunteer hours available to the church's mission and the locale for the work of the church in the lives of those far from God. In chapter 4 we describe the individual aspects of CBSE by explaining the key concepts of "community," "based," "servant," and "evangelism."

Chapter 5 describes those who do the work of CBSE, the salt and light servants. These Christ-followers are engaged in their communities as the end picture of what a local church seeks to develop by its equipping ministries. Salt and light servants are Matthew 5:13–16 disciples of Jesus who take up the towel of service to meet the needs of those around them in the name of Jesus. Chapter 6 describes the "connection points" through which salt and light servants share the love of Christ. These experiences have also been called "bridges of influence" in which the church gains a hearing among those served in the name of Jesus.

Chapters 7 and 8 provide the process through which you can lead your church to practice CBSE. This eleven-step process is the plan–from God's prompting to mobilizing your church into the community as salt and light servants. Appendices with tools to aid in leading your church to live out the Great Commandment and Great Commission complete our resource for you.

We are as confident as ever that the church is God's way of redeeming creation back to Himself. While there is much to be concerned about with the church in North America, we see glimpses of a new movement of Christ-followers returning to the place of their calling in the name of the one who called them. Our prayer is that this leadership resource can aid you as you follow Jesus into the community where He had placed you.

Steve Pate, D.Min.

C. Gene Wilkes, Ph.D.

Notes

[1]Alan Roxburgh, *The Missionary Congregation* (Harrisburg, Pa.: Trinity Press International, 1997), and id., *The Missional Leader* (San Francisco: Jossey-Bass, 2006).

[2]Eddie Gibbs and Ryan Bolger, *Emerging Churches: Creating Christian Communities in Postmodern Cultures* (Grand Rapids: Baker Books, 2005).

1

Foundations

Community-Based Servant Evangelism

Take a brief survey today as you move from task to task. Ask the person in the next office, the first person to stop and talk for a moment, the store clerk, your boss, the first five people who smile at you. No qualifications for this survey. Just ask ten people.

The questions?

Just one: What do you and people you associate with think about _____(*name of your church*). Be sure people do not just put a nice spin on their answers. Get the real consensus about your church.

Using these answers, you see the work your church has to do among the people you associate with every day. Now you see the need for your church to want to be missional–that is, reach beyond itself to accomplish God's mission where you live.

Now you are ready to read this book.

How can your church create a missional environment? How can your church re-engage its community through servant evangelism?

No great secrets here, just some tried and true foundational concepts. These pivot around basic definitions and issues: the functional meanings of *evangelism* and *mission,* the importance and understanding of *salvation,* a model for *outreach,* a unique salvation presentation. We want to help you understand some of the barriers that naturally keep your church within the walls of the buildings and captured by program maintenance. These include time (or lack thereof), a lack of appreciation for the passion and spiritual gifts of members, and your church structures.

Ineffective Methods

Historically, evangelicals have recognized the importance of evangelism and evangelistic training. Lifeway Press, Next Gen (Cook Communications), Zondervan, Campus Crusade, NavPress, plus many individual churches have produced evangelism-training materials to motivate and equip members to share their faith. The majority of the training models encourage people to make a personal visit to a home in the hope that they may lead those in that place into a relationship with Christ. Despite the zeal with which many churches have approached evangelism, their effectiveness falls short of expectations. Why?

Today's church leadership must answer a critical question. Why, after training tens of thousands of our church members to share their faith, are evangelism results so low and continuing to decline? The training materials by and large have been good. Therefore, the production of "new and improved" training materials is not the answer, except for denominational agencies and publishers. Maybe the evangelism trainers could somehow teach the material better, therefore resulting in more Christ-followers sharing their faith. However, the improvement of the trainers most likely would only result in incremental changes. What the churches in the U.S. need are exponential changes!

Many Christians have read the Great Commission so often that they either zone out because they have heard it so often, or they think the challenge is so large their efforts would do little to reach "all nations." We believe the majority of church members want to see their friends and neighbors come to Christ, but most are frustrated when asked, "When was the last time you shared your faith with someone?"

On the other hand, when asked, "What is God up to in your life?" they can say much about God's presence in their lives. When the focus moves from one's duty and training as a church member to one's personal relationship with God, people have something to talk about.

Confrontational or direct evangelism was successful when many people had some biblical foundation for moral justice or eternal consequences. However, today most people have no biblical knowledge when the conversation begins, much less a biblical worldview that presupposes living under a moral code with eternal consequences. We now must spend more time defending the reliability of the Bible and confessing the historical sins of the Church and organized religion than we do helping people deal with the spiritual guilt of their sins.

What the church has done can amount to what the Texas Rangers baseball team has done through the years: change the manager, build a state-of-the-art ballpark, and change the uniforms from red to blue and now back to red. I (Steve) am a die-hard St. Louis Cardinal fan. The Cardinals have won ten "world championships"; the Texas Rangers, zero. The problems the Rangers have are the leaders and the players. The culture is not conducive to winning.

Churches have tried changes like those of the Texas Rangers, and they have resulted in minimal improvement at best. Much of the solution, we believe, lies in realigning the culture, values, and methodology of the local church.

Societal mores and models for how we live together have changed. In suburban America, for example, some people live in gated communities, thus eliminating "cold calls" for evangelism. Most new homes do not have a front porch, nor is the front door anything more than a way to the mailbox or a place to hang doorknob advertisements. Instead, homes have electrically powered garage doors, which drivers activate from inside their cars. Neighbors may go days or weeks without speaking or even seeing one another. The time-honored approach of engaging a stranger or acquaintance at his or her home can no longer be the only approach to helping people trust Jesus.

George Barna, after surveying the unchurched, concluded:

> The key revelation is that there must be multiple routes of entry available to unchurched people. The greatest influence would be for a friend to invite the unchurched person to accompany them [*sic*] to church: two-thirds of the unchurched said that would have a positive effect.[1]

Friendship or web evangelism (back when "web" meant your network of relationships, not the Internet) has been around for some time, and Barna's data supports this methodology for helping people trust Jesus. What about the local church as a whole? How do you engage your congregation to mobilize to engage the mission field in which it is planted? If we are to fulfill the Great Commission, people must go where people are and invite them to "the feast" (Lk. 14:23). Multiple connection points enable members to build authentic relationships with people far from God.

The premise of this book is simple: the key for a local church is to create natural connection points for Christ-followers to intersect the lives of people far from God through service in the community as salt and light servants.

Why Aren't Our Efforts Producing Anything Other Than More Work?

The Denton Baptist Association, for which Steve is a consultant, decided to focus its resources and personnel on evangelism for a season. The results of that focus have been somewhat varied. The number of baptisms increased from 1896 in the year 1999 to 2100 in the year 2003. However, after careful examination, of those 2100 baptisms, 12 percent were denominational baptisms (Christ-followers who were not previously immersed); 54 percent were biological (children or grandchildren of members) and 34 percent were conversions (individuals with no prior connection to a church).[2]

Additionally, looking at the percentage of church members within the Denton County population, the Denton Association has seen a decline from 4.3 percent of the population in 1999 to 1.9% in 2003. This decline has taken place at the same time church membership has risen nearly 10,000 since 1999! The demographic information has also shown an increase in the ethnic population of Denton County.[3] The numerical church growth does not indicate progress in reaching Denton County for Christ.

Ron S. Lewis, our mentor and longtime church consultant, observed, "Process precedes product. What you are doing, and how you are doing it, determines the results."[4] Church outreach programs, age-grouped Bible studies, church-wide evangelistic emphases and events have produced the current results. If churches desire a different end result, the process must change!

Some churches plateau or decline simply because they have become comfortable. They like things the way they are. They have forgotten that the Christian church is not simply to be a safe house for members, where we are to withdraw, keeping any possibility of evil and danger away at all cost. As William Shedd, the nineteenth-century theologian, noted, "A ship in harbor is safe, but that is not what ships are built for." A study of Paul's ministry illustrates a life on mission is anything other than channel surfing from a recliner.[5] Ron Martoia quipped, "If the church isn't living on the edge, it's taking up way too much space."[6]

Your answers to these questions may help: How close to the edge is your church? If you are comfortable, what intentional steps can you take to position your church back where it belongs, back on the edge?

Another reason evangelism fails is that churches ask people to fill positions in existing ministries regardless of their passions or spiritual gifts. We too often forget the organic picture of the church is a body, not an organization chart. The Holy Spirit has already equipped each member of that body with at least one gift to serve the common good of the whole (1 Cor. 12:7, 12). The Holy Spirit gives spiritual gifts to Christ-followers to build up the body (Eph. 4:11). Most evangelism training courses overlook the giftedness of members and offer a "one-size-fits-all" presentation that each disciple must master and then recite to others. Spiritual gifts indicate "what" you will do when you serve.[7] We have seen those with the spiritual gift of evangelism be most effective in reaching those far from God.

Passion answers the "where" question of ministry. We believe God has written on the heart of every Christ-follower a passionate desire to serve Him. When a person finds that passion, that person begins to serve out of that "sweet spot" and find the greatest joy in his or her lives. Passion is the nuclear reactor that generates an energy that never burns out. Service is how one begins to discover one's passion. Bill Hybels wrote, "Use whatever understanding you have of your passions, areas of interest, and gifts to guide you in a general serving direction. Look at the needs in your church and community. Then jump in with a willing heart and an open mind. Drape a servant's towel over your arm, and get busy."[8] Churches should ask the important question: "Aside from your work, what is it you really like to do?"[9] By asking such a question to volunteers, you will discover the Holy Spirit can move people into action much better than can a staff member who must fill an open slot.

Questions you may answer are: "What new things does God want to do in us and through us?"[10] What have we done in the past and are doing now that produces the current results? If you want to change your results, you must not only answer the questions but also implement changes to realize new outcomes.

Here is one way to get started. The Old Testament prophecy of Micah (Mic. 6:8) outlines three areas you can address to embrace change in your church for the cause of Christ. God "requires" of you to "walk humbly with God (personal salvation, spiritual disciplines, and worship), love mercy (acts of kindness, meeting basic human needs) and act justly (addresses causes that create systems)."[11] To walk humbly with God means to trust His Son and Rescuer and Leader and follow the ways of God as the pattern for living. To love people into a relationship with Jesus is the basis for biblical evangelism. Acts of intentional (not random) kindness and meeting basic human needs lead the *ekklesia* into the community to serve people in the name of Jesus. To act justly means to actively engage "the rulers...the authorities... the powers of this dark world and...the spiritual forces of evil in the heavenly realms" (Eph. 6:12, NIV) in the name of Jesus wherever injustice occurs. This is more than registering voters for the next presidential election. It means engaging the systems that cause poverty, inequality, and prejudice among people. Each of these areas forms the beginning of CBSE. What would happen if you led your church into the community to live out the "requirements" God has given His people? Robert Lewis, pastor of Fellowship Bible Church, Little Rock, Arkansas, led his church to ask and answer several key questions:

> Can you imagine the community in which you live being genuinely thankful for your Church? Can you imagine city leaders valuing your church's friendship and participation in the community–even asking for it? Can you imagine a large number of your church members actively engaged in, and passionate about, community service, using their gifts and abilities in ways and at levels, they never thought possible? Can you imagine the spiritual harvest that would naturally follow if all of this were true?[12]

Churches can deploy their members according to their passions and gifts to be an irresistible influence among the people of their community. Church members can find in the body of Christ the place they were created to belong and function. Volunteers serving in hospitals, U.S. Customs offices, nursing homes, community shelters, homes for unwed mothers, and community recreation programs can create a church that the entire community not only appreciates, but, more importantly, a church that actually fulfils the Great Commission–and in spontaneous and natural ways.

Great Commandment or Great Commission?

Many churches across America struggle for their identities and to understand God's vision for their churches. They struggle with methods, programs, and strategies implemented to fulfill their visions. They struggle with their organizational structures, budgets, the percentage of the church budgets devoted to church staff, and members giving tithes and offerings. However, could we not all agree that the area in which the local church struggles most is its attempt to fulfill *both* the Great Commission and the Great Commandment? Here they are as recorded in Scripture:

> "Go therefore and make disciples of all the nations, baptizing them in the name of the Father and the Son and the Holy Spirit, teaching them to observe all that I commanded you; and lo, I am with you always, even to the end of the age." (Mt 28:19–20)

> "'You shall love the Lord your God with all your heart, and with all your soul, and with all your mind.' This is the great and foremost commandment. The second is like it, 'You shall love your neighbor as yourself.'" (Mt 22:37–40)

We are confident that many of the issues churches struggle with would be alleviated if churches made the Great Commission and the Great Commandment the foci of their efforts. These Christ-commands are the heart of our mission as Christ-followers. They are the foundations of spiritual formation that should be the core processes upon which our churches function. Dallas Willard states, "Spiritual formation in Christ is the process leading to that ideal end, and its result is love of God with all of the heart, soul, mind, and strength, and of the neighbor as oneself."[13]

In the process of continued ministry and research for this book, we have adjusted our theology, philosophy, and methodology of ministry. For years if you were to ask us to list the Great Commission and Great Commandment in order of priority, we would have both said the Great Commission had priority over the Great Commandment as it relates to the mission of the church. Had we missed the obvious? When asked what the most important commandment was, Jesus responded with an affirmation of God's direction to Israel (Deut. 6:4; Mk. 12:30). He had the chance to spin the vision for the Great Commission to be primary in the lives of His followers, but He chose loving God and loving others as the most important.

You can argue that Jesus affirmed the *Shema prior* to his resurrection and commissioned his disciples to go into all the world *after* it, and that we cannot lean on that order because one belongs to His fulfillment of the Old Covenant and the other involves the establishment of a New Covenant. However, Jesus said He came to "fulfill" the first Covenant and not to abolish it (Mt. 5:17). Jesus had commissioned His disciples already to go and tell others about the kingdom of Heaven (Mt. 10), but when asked the supreme law for all people, He answered with the greatest commandment: love God, love others.

John reminds us, "We love, because [God] first loved us," and adds, "The one who loves God should love his brother also" (1 Jn. 4:19, 21). The love of God is our motivation as Christ-followers to love our "brothers" and to complete the Great Commission. If we do not love God with all our heart, soul, strength, and mind, and love people with the love of God in us, why should we care about people heading toward a Christ-less eternity? The Great Commandment *motivates* us to do whatever we can to see those we have relationships with begin a personal walk with Christ. Paul reminds us that if Christlike love is not the inspiration for our evangelization, we are nothing but a "noisy gong or a clanging cymbal" (1 Cor. 13:1b). The love of Christ, which transforms our hearts to love others, motivates us to action. Acts of random kindness or meeting physical needs without God's serving love will not result in kingdom growth. Christ made it clear that His followers were to love God and to love others while going about life helping people trust Jesus.

Erwin McManus says it like this:

> When Jesus was asked what was the greatest of all the commandments, he was essentially being asked what is the most important thing to God. His answer could be summarized in one word: relationships. Essentially all the church is, is relationships. Without relationships, the church ceases to exist. Relationship to God and relationship to others are what the church is all about.[14]

Another way to emphasize this is that our job as church leaders is to assist people to live at the intersection of the vertical and horizontal wooden beams of the cross; the vertical represents our personal relationship with Christ, and the horizontal represents our community relationships with people. The Great Commandment creates that intersection where CBSE can become a strategy to complete the Great Commission.

Salt and Light Evangelism

We remember when, as church-going children, evangelists and pastors challenged us to find a Bible verse or passage that gave us a pass on sharing our faith. We knew by the way they asked the question the search would be futile, so, we went back to passing notes to our friends. As maturing followers of Jesus, we know a Christ-follower must share the gospel message. The apostle Paul asked, "How then will they call on Him in whom they have not believed? How will they believe in Him whom they have not heard? And how will they hear without a preacher?" (Rom. 10:14). Steve Ayers observed, "We'll never see people become a part of the bride of Christ until we ask them to."[15]

So, what is the best way to help people trust Jesus when we are called to love others and invite them to become part of the bride of Christ? In what we call the Sermon on the Mount, Jesus asked His followers to live in such a way that others may see what they did and give credit to His Father in Heaven. He said:

> "You are the salt of the earth; but if the salt has become tasteless, how can it be made salty again? It will no longer be good for anything, except to be thrown out and trampled under foot by men. You are the light of the world. A city set on a hill cannot be hidden... Let your light shine before men in such a way that they may see your good works, and glorify your Father who is in heaven." (Mt. 5: 13–14, 16)

"Christians have not been placed here to curse the darkness, but to be salt and light. We cannot expect the world to reflect our values unless we have first reached them with the love and message of Christ,"[16] comment two prominent preachers. Is this how Jesus taught His disciples to do evangelism? We think so, and call His strategy "Salt and Light Evangelism."

What do the metaphors of "salt" and "light" mean? Salt does several things. It makes people thirsty. This image suggests Christ-followers are to live lives that demonstrate a sense of purpose, peace, and joy. By living this type of spiritual life, a thirst for spiritual things would develop among the people who were far from God, and be served by those who followed Jesus. He said in another context, "He who loves his life loses it, and he who hates his life in this world shall keep it to life eternal. If anyone serves Me, he must follow Me; and where I am, there My servant will be also; if anyone serves Me, the Father will honor him" (Jn. 12:25–26).

Salt can also enhance food's flavor as a spice. Jesus' followers add flavor to the lives of people who were far from Him. How? By living a lives that are authentic and bold in their faith. Christ's disciples add spices of celebration and consistency during tough circumstances. They find hope when others have given up.

Salt can also preserve. When Christ-followers live the type of life that demonstrates God's love for the world, they can affect the moral fiber of the culture. God can use His followers to stem the downward moral slide of culture. Christ-followers should be a positive influence for God in their communities as they live a life reflective of "love, joy, peace, patience, kindness, goodness, faithfulness, gentleness, [and] self-control" (Gal. 5:22b–23a).

Why is the salt metaphor important to a discussion about evangelism? Mark Mittelberg and Bill Hybels observe:

> First, in order for salt to have the greatest possible impact, it must be potent enough to have an effect. And second, for any impact to take place, salt has to get close to whatever it is supposed to affect. So Jesus may have chosen the salt metaphor because salt requires both potency and proximity to do its thing.[17]

Jesus gave His followers the salt metaphor for application among the non-kingdom people, not for those inside.

Likewise, Christ-followers must apply the light metaphor as influencing those outside the church, among people who are facing a Christ-less eternity. "A city set on a hill cannot be hidden" (Mt. 5:14b). A church filled with the light of God's love and love for others cannot be hidden behind stain-glassed walls. "Nor," Jesus added, "does anyone light a lamp and put it under a basket, but on the lampstand, and it gives light to all who are in the house" (5:15). Light benefits both those who are outside the city and those "in the house." What are we to do as light? Jesus concluded, "Let your light shine before men in such a way that they may see your good works, and glorify your Father who is in heaven" (5:16). God will get the credit for our good works when we reflect His nature in our "good works."

The deployment of people in the world is exactly what Jesus had in mind as he gave them these pictures for their lives. Jesus was passionate about seeing His followers out in the world as salt and light. Shortly before He was arrested and crucified, Jesus prayed these words for them:

> "I do not ask You to take them out of the world, but to keep them from the evil one. They are not of the world, even as I am not of the world. Sanctify them in the truth; Your word is truth. As You sent Me into the world, I also have sent them into the world." (Jn. 17:15–18)

Jesus wanted His followers to rub shoulders with real people, both the poor and the rich. His strategy was not to force anyone to trust Him, but He patiently engaged anyone who came to Him.

Michael Simpson describes Jesus' encounter with the rich young ruler this way:

> Christ was evangelizing, but it sure doesn't look like the way most people do it today. Even though it says Jesus loved him, he stood there and let the man walk away. Why did Christ not follow him when he walked away? Why didn't He try harder when this man seemed so eager? Why didn't Jesus "get him saved" before addressing this difficult area of his life? Christ's approach was first to weed out the willing seekers and then go deeper with them. He promised hope over pain. He condemned sin, not the sinner. He never attacked; he invited. Love is a choice, so it can never be forced and genuine at the same time. Salvation is choosing the ultimate expression of love and adheres to the same rules. Christ's approach is based on His equal desire for love and His respect for the gift of free will. When looking for a spouse, one woos. Threats are never the basis for a healthy relationship.[18]

Mittelberg and Hybels conclude, "Jesus was accused by His enemies of being a friend of tax collectors and 'sinners' (Luke 7:34). Though this was meant to be a derogatory term, Jesus never denied it. Instead, He took it as a compliment and actively embodied it."[19] Jesus did not mind being addressed as a friend of sinners.

The local church must purposefully deploy people into the community, becoming friends of sinners, if Christ-followers are to live out this verse and the Great Commission. Ron Lewis stated, "We need to develop our love for our neighbors and friends to the point we cannot stand the thought of them being separated from God for eternity. That will motivate us to do everything possible to see them come into a saving relationship with Christ."[20] Our love for God (loving God with all our heart, mind, soul, and strength) should compel us to love our neighbor.

Salt and light have their greatest impact outside the local church:

> Christ didn't just hang out with sinners; He initiated contact, enjoyed their presence, accepted their gifts, and publicly defended them. He let them know that He sympathized with the plight of the impact from their sins, but never condoned those sins, participated in them, or hid His concern. Christ went to great lengths to let the lost know He understood them, honored them, and had their best interests in mind even to the point of death.[21]

The Pharisees and scribes did not like the type of people Jesus chose to be with. Religious law separated the "insiders" from the "outsiders." One reason the religious leaders nailed Jesus to the tree was because He loved to hang with people whose reputations were subpar, whose professions were "filthy," whose bodies was diseased, and whose lives did not fit the mold of the religiously correct.

The local church must understand the eternal implications of continuing business as is. The church must re-engage the people in their community and ministry fields. According to Bill Easum, "The focus is how the church can be leaven and salt in the community around it and throughout the world. The church is no longer the place where religious things happen, but the launch pad from which cross-cultural witnesses are sent out into the world."[22]

Beyond Salt and Light

Let's examine another biblical illustration of community-based evangelism. In 2 Kings 6–7, the Bible describes a siege and resulting famine that affected the entire city of Jerusalem. The situation was so dire that a woman proposed to another woman that they eat the other woman's son on that day, and then eat her son tomorrow. God's plan, however, was to utilize four lepers to break the famine.

Now, the Law prohibited lepers from living among healthy members of the tribe. The diseased people were to live away from others so they would not infect others with their disease (Num. 5:1–3).

The four lepers considered every possibility to save themselves. If they stayed where they were, they would surely die. If they returned to the city, they would also die. They chose to go to the enemy camp and beg for food. In a worst-case scenario their enemies would turn them away or kill them.

The Bible says when they arrived at the enemy camp, it was empty. The enemy had abandoned everything and fled. The four lepers went from tent to tent hoarding their newly found bounty. The Bible says that after a while, the lepers came to their senses and remembered those in the city who were starving to death. "We are not doing right. This day is a day of good news, but we are keeping silent; if we wait until morning light, punishment will overtake us. Now therefore come, let us go and tell the king's household" (2 Kings 7:9).

Although the lepers had more than enough for themselves and could have argued how unjustly everyone back home had treated them and did not deserve their treasure trove, they decided to go tell others about what they had found. Isn't evangelism mostly lepers who have been outcast sharing the bounty they have stumbled upon with friends and family?

Ron Lewis said many times, "People will spend eternity somewhere."[23] Just the thought of the eternal punishment that acquaintances, friends, and family face should motivate all Christians to share the Good News with those starving for God's love. Christ-followers hoarding or hiding the Good News is exactly what Christ cautioned His followers about when He said, "Nor does anyone light a lamp and put it under a basket, but on the lampstand, and it gives light to all who are in the house" (Mt. 5:15).

Consider also the story of a paralytic and his friends (Lk. 5:17–26). The paralytic's friends loved him so much they carried him on a mat to Jesus with the hope the man might physically be healed. When they arrived, Luke tells us, they found the crowd so large there that it would be difficult to complete the vision they had for their paraplegic friend. The paralytic's friends determined that the only way to accomplish their goal was to enter the house through the roof. The men climbed on the roof, removed a section of the ceiling, and lowered their friend on his mat in front of Jesus. Luke records, "Seeing their faith, He said, 'Friend, your sins are forgiven you'" (Lk. 5:20). The Pharisees who heard Jesus' pronouncement talked among themselves, saying that Jesus was blaspheming God, because only God can forgive sins.

Jesus replied:

> "Why are you reasoning in your hearts? Which is easier, to say, 'Your sins have been forgiven you,' or to say, 'Get up and walk'? But, so that you may know that the Son of Man has authority on earth to forgive sins,"–He said to the paralytic–"I say to you, get up, and pick up your stretcher and go home." Immediately he got up before them, and picked up what he had been lying on, and went home, glorifying God. (Lk. 5:22b–25)

This story contains two aspects of CBSE: (1) develop authentic relationships with people far from God; and (2) seize an opportunity to meet a need, thereby helping to bring them to Jesus. Christ-followers connect people to Jesus as they meet needs in the midst of developing authentic relationships.

What is the goal of our evangelism? How do we distinguish what we talk about from other forms of community service and servant evangelism? When can we declare our efforts effective and by what measure?

The Goal and Content of Community-Based
Servant Evangelism

Evangelism is simply to "tell the Good News" to others. We suggest churches "tell" the story of Jesus through meeting needs in their communities in the name of Jesus. We do not offer a presentation to be memorized but a lifestyle of service that engages tangible needs wherever they may occur and seizes every opportunity in that interaction to introduce the person/people served to our Rescuer and Leader, Jesus. The outcome of our mission is the miraculous transformation of a person's life through a relationship with Jesus Christ. We echo David Bosch's prophetic words, "Mission therefore means being involved in the ongoing dialogue between God, who offers his salvation, and the world, which—enmeshed in all kinds of evil—craves that salvation."[24]

Today, many people believe if they do more good than bad, that alone will gain them entrance into heaven. However, if God's nature were not both holy and loving, the fall of man would have spelled the end of the short story of humankind. Gilbert Bilezikian has concluded, "Having been held in contempt by his creatures, God had every right to abandon them to the destructive power of Satan. He could have turned his back on the human situation and let it rot into fine dust."[25] We need to be reminded from time to time that God created humans out of His love and that God saves them because of His love. The apostle Paul declared, "But God demonstrates His love toward us, in that while we were yet sinners, Christ died for us" (Rom. 5:8). The love of God is a love *demonstrated* in relationship, and those who love as does God, revealed in Christ Jesus, *demonstrate* that same love to others.

CBSE relates directly to the teaching of Jesus when He commanded His followers to go and make disciples of all people, informing people how much they matter to the Father (Mt. 28:18–20). That should become a focus of our lives as we love God and love others (Mt. 22:37–39). The major responsibilities for all Christ-followers are contained in both of these passages. "In short, we must return to simple delight in the Lord and respectful sorrow for the lost. When we are amazed again at the work of God in our own lives, we cease to suppress the Holy Spirit. When the Holy Spirit is free and evident in our lives, God draws people to us. Then, and only then, will we be effective in evangelism."[26]

Christ said, "And you shall love the Lord your God with all your heart and with all your soul and with all your mind and with all your strength" (Mk. 12:30). In addition to such singularly focused love for

God, Christ-followers are to love others because Jesus said that the world would know if someone was a follower of His by their love for one another (Jn. 13:35). "On these two commandments depend the whole law and the Prophets" (Mt. 22:40). The "love God" and "love others" command is the action necessary to fulfill Christ's Great Commission. The result of following the command of loving God and loving people motivates Christ-followers to share the gospel message with family members, friends, and neighbors.

The Essence of the Good News

As we have said, the goal of CBSE is changed lives through an ongoing relationship with Jesus. That relationship is founded on the biblical realities of who God is, who people are, the resulting separation by sinful acts, and God's gracious gift of reconciliation through His Son, Jesus. Without this message in the demonstration of Christlike love, our acts of service no longer find themselves in the mission of the church. So, what is that kernel of the Good News, the *kerygma* of our actions?

The gospel message is first about God. God is love (1 Jn. 4:16). God is holy and absolutely pure (1 Pet. 1:16). God is also just; He is a good and perfect judge (2 Thess. 1:6). On the other hand, the Bible says that man is sinful (Rom. 3:23). On their own, people are spiritually helpless to do anything about the issue sin creates (Isa. 64:6). The result of the sinful condition is that man deserves death, both a physical and spiritual death (Rom. 6:23).

Christ did something for people they could never do for themselves. First, Christ became God *incarnate*, in flesh (Jn. 1:1, 14). The Bible teaches Jesus is God's only Son, who came to earth so man might spend eternity with God in Heaven (Jn. 3:16). Jesus also died as a substitute sacrifice on the behalf of all people (1 Pet. 2:24). He offers forgiveness as a free gift (Eph. 2:8–9).

Nevertheless, it is not enough to know all of this. The Bible says, "You believe that God is one. You do well; the demons also believe, and shudder" (Jam. 2:19). God asks us to respond. "But as many as received Him, to them He gave the right to become children of God, even to those who believe in His name" (Jn. 1:12). People must also ask Christ to be their Forgiver and Leader (1 Jn. 1:9). The result for people is a spiritual transformation. "Therefore if anyone is in Christ, he is a new creature; the old things passed away; behold, new things have come" (2 Cor. 5:17).[27] Jesus locked eyes with people who were "distressed and dispirited" like sheep without a shepherd (Mt. 9:36).

CBSE is motivated by God's rescuing love toward people and contains the life-changing message of Jesus Christ. The love of God in response to His love for us in Christ Jesus motivates us to go in the name of Jesus to all people to serve them as He served us.

QUESTIONS FOR CONSIDERATION

1. Take a look at your last one hundred new church members. How many came as already "convinced"? As children of members? How many came as the result of members inviting a person far from God and the person becoming a Christ-follower?
2. In what tangible ways is your church today living on the edge?
3. How many of your church members currently serving in church programs, ministries, and events are mismatched with their passion and spiritual gifting?
4. Is the Great Commandment your foundational Scripture for all your church's evangelistic efforts? Do your members clearly understand that to love God fully they must love "others," and that if they authentically love "others" they must love God? What steps must be taken to help your church operate by the Great Commandment?
5. Are you (*church leader*) modeling a "Salt and Light" life? If not, what are your next steps?
6. Can your members clearly articulate the essence of the gospel message?
7. Are your members so personally engaged with the Father that they have current examples of what God is doing in their lives?

Notes

[1]George Barna, *Re-Churching the Unchurched* (Ventura: Issachar Resources, 2000), 104.

[2]Annual report of churches of the Denton Baptist Association.

[3]Percept, Ministry Area Profile 2003 Compass Report, Study Area Definition: Denton County Texas: ID # 29095:63591.

[4]Personal notes from Ron S. Lewis, used by permission.

[5]C. Gene Wilkes, *Paul on Leadership: Servant Leadership in a Ministry of Transition* (Nashville: LifeWay, 2004), 80–101.

[6]Ron Martoia, *Morph!* (Loveland: Group Publishing, 2003), 159.

[7]Bruce Bugbee, Don Cousins, and Bill Hybels, *Network: Leader's Guide* (Grand Rapids: Zondervan, 1994), 46.

[8]Bill Hybels, *Volunteers* (Grand Rapids: Zondervan, 2004), 71.

[9]Bill Hybels, The Leadership Summit 2004, *The Leader's Edge,* Session 2, CD.

[10]Martoia, *Morph!,* 124.

[11]Rick Rusaw and Eric Swanson, *The Externally Focused Church* (Loveland: Group Publishing, 2004), 137.

[12]Robert Lewis and Rob Wilkins, *The Church of Irresistible Influence* (Grand Rapids: Zondervan, 2001) 13–14.

[13]Dallas Willard, *Renovation of the Heart* (Colorado Springs: NavPress, 2002), 114.

[14]Erwin Raphael McManus, *An Unstoppable Force* (Loveland: Group Publishing, 2001), 158.

[15]Steve Ayers, *Igniting Passion in Your Church* (Loveland: Group Publishing, 2003), 42.

[16]Ted Haggard and Jack Hayford, *Loving Your City into the Kingdom* (Ventura: Regal, 1997), 156.

[17]Mark Mittelberg and Bill Hybels, *Becoming a Contagious Christian* (Grand Rapids: Zondervan, 1994), 42.

[18]Michael L. Simpson, *Permission Evangelism* (Colorado Springs: Cook Communication Ministries, 2003), 51.

[19]Mittelberg and Hybels, *Becoming a Contagious Christian,* 101.

[20]Ron S. Lewis, used by permission.

[21]Simpson, *Permission Evangelism,* 128.

[22]Bill Easum, *Leadership on the Other Side* (Nashville: Abingdon Press, 2000), 122.

[23]Ron S. Lewis, used by permission.

[24]Donald. J. Bosch, *Transforming Mission* (New York: Orbis Books, 1991), 400.

[25]Gilbert Bilezikian, *Christianity 101* (Grand Rapids: Zondervan, 1993), 143.

[26]Simpson, *Permission Evangelism,* 77.

[27]See Mark Mittelberg, *Becoming a Contagious Christian, Participants Guide* (Grand Rapids: Zondervan, 1995), 60–63.

2

Barriers That Keep Us Out of Our Communities

Barriers, both perceived and tangible, prevent churches from living out the Great Commandment and the Great Commission. Randy Frazee calculates that the average American family engages in thirteen commutes a day, that 80 percent of the cars on the road have one person in them, and that the average stay-at-home mom or dad spends up to six hours a day running errands.[1] According to Frazee, our lives produce a "crowded loneliness," which isolates us from relationships that are essential for both the Great Commandment and Great Commission. We just don't have time for anything else in our lives.

I (Gene) heard Kennon Callahan say once, "We have taught our people to make decisions, not make disciples." He meant we have trained churched people to populate our institutional committees and make decisions for others about how they can use God's resources rather than equipping them to "love a friend to Jesus," grow her into the likeness of Christ, and send her back into her own mission field to help her friends trust Jesus. How we do church is a barrier to mobilizing people to co-mission with Christ in the mission fields of our communities.

Mark Hagan has the spiritual gift of giving and a passion to serve battered women in the Dallas area. Mark and his wife, Edie, live out of their passion and giftedness to provide transformational housing and a two-year path to wholeness for women and single moms in the name of Jesus. They are the founders and drive behind Dallas Providence Homes, which has two homes running at the time of this publication, and which has a goal of having ten homes in operation by 2010.[2] Mark and Edie serve their local church's ministries, but most of their time is spent on this vital community ministry to which they call people from all walks of life to serve those in need. By doing so, they meet a significant community need while mobilizing Christ-followers and others to join them.

Time (or a perceived lack of time), program maintenance, church structures, and unawareness of passion and spiritual gifts among the members of your church are primary barriers that keep your people out of the community and within the walls of your church. We want to address these barriers and offer some ideas of how to overcome them.

The Barrier of Time

While visiting with many pastors and staff members across America, I (Steve) have repeatedly heard that the number one barrier they deal with is (lack of) time. Success drives many to pack their personal schedules. Hectic lifestyles stem from the desire to climb the corporate ladder one more rung, to get just one more important thing completed, or to become better off financially. Ray Oldenberg has observed, "The thought of devoting additional time and effort to the establishment of…a community life more generally, can be a discouraging one. Time and energy are commodities that too many of us have too little of to spare."[3] This can escalate to the point that someone who cares a great deal about us might say, "If you don't watch out, success could kill you."[4] With all the conveniences of life and with all the technological advances, why is time management such an issue? We agree with the futurist, David Zach, who has described our condition of overcommitment as "hyperliving–skimming along the surface of life."[5]

Many have thought technological advancements would allow us to finally "de-stress" our hectic lives. Progress was supposed to add margin in our lives. In the 1950s and 1960s many thought that by the time the year 2000 rolled around, we would be grasping for things and events to fill up our days. Progress has instead consumed more of our time, not less. According to research by Richard Swenson, M.D., over fifteen years ago, "For every hour progress saves by organizing and technologizing our time, it consumes two more hours through the consequences, direct or indirect, of this activity."[6] Imagine what the technological impact on time is now!

Stephen R. Covey, a sage of highly effective habits, observed, "As a longtime student of this fascinating field, I am personally persuaded that the essence of the best thinking in the area of time management can be captured in a single phrase: organize and execute around priorities."[7] Covey believes everything fits into one of four quadrants: urgent and important, urgent and not important, not urgent and important, and finally not urgent and not important. We generally make decisions in areas perceived to be in the urgent and important quadrant first, with progressively less attention paid to making decisions in each of the other quadrants, down through the not urgent and not important quadrant, delaying or even putting off indeterminately some decisions. Now, where does this then leave Jesus' "Greatest Commandment" and "Great Commission" in our lives? Well, unless our relationship with Jesus is considered "urgent *and* important," we most likely will continue to defer our time choices to what we consider more "urgent and important," or even more "urgent and not important" things of life.

We must confess that the leadership of the local church is often responsible for adding stress to members' lives. Many churches have far too many time-consuming programs, events, and meetings each week that do not enable their church to move even one step forward in accomplishing the two "Great C's" of our followership of Christ. We put our best people in maintenance of the institution rather than mobilized on mission. With only so many hours in a day and members already overcommitted, we do not suggest a message series on time management to solve the problem, but rather a different way of calculating what you ask your people to do to carry out the work of your church.

Try treating the person-hours that members and volunteers give to the church and the Lord with the same intentionality you treat every dollar contributed to the church. You create, monitor, adjust, and raise funds to have the financial resources for your ministry. Why not do the same with the number of volunteer hours required to complete your ministries? You know your per capita giving and what it takes to sustain your ministries, staff, and facilities. Do you know the number of "person-hours" needed to sustain what you have asked your people to do?

Try this calculation with this simple formula:

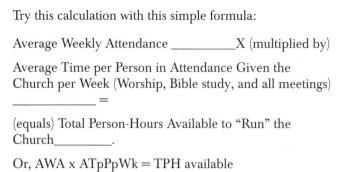

Average Weekly Attendance _____X (multiplied by)

Average Time per Person in Attendance Given the
Church per Week (Worship, Bible study, and all meetings)
_____ =

(equals) Total Person-Hours Available to "Run" the
Church_____.

Or, AWA x ATpPpWk = TPH available

For example, if a church's average attendance is 100 and the average amount of time given by each of the 100 people (including all preschool and children) is 2.5 hours per week, the church has 250 person-hours to "run" the church. Subtract 100 hours for worship attendance and another 85 for Bible study attendance and that leaves 65 person-hours remaining. The key question is where are you as a church going to invest the remaining 65 hours that gives you the best shot at fulfilling the Great Commandment and the Great Commission? Other questions including: Is there a way you can leverage worship and Bible study to have a greater influence for the Kingdom? What activities, events, demands, or expectations may be wasting the person-hours your members contribute to your church?

Church leadership must become as tenacious about the expenditure of person-hours as we currently are about the expenditure of church finances. If a church is serious about the investment of person-hours, your intensity of evaluation should be the same as that which is applied to each dollar designated in the church's annual budget.

The Church Program Barrier

Those of us who serve a local church know that programs and programming is how most of us currently do church. Plain and simple, the success of our programs determines the success of our ministries. We count the "Four B's" (Budgets, Buildings, Baptisms, and Bodies) each week as our gauge of success. Associations and denominations keep up with these tangible markers to evaluate members' health and well-being. A few have figured out how to gauge the success of a church program by looking at the program's leadership. The key questions are: How many are there? Are they trained? A fewer number count the number of new programs started and/or new church program ideas implemented.

Programs are not inherently bad. They represent the ways in which you carry out your church's essential mission. It's *how* we treat them that makes the difference. Programs in the church are no different than any other aspect in our lives. We must ask: Are they the tail that wags the dog? We have created programs to assist the local church to fulfill its mission and vision, not the church to fulfill the programs' requirements and resources.

To correct our misunderstanding of church programs in the twenty-first century, we must first understand how programs have taken on a life of their own. Church programs have created several issues in local churches.

1. Programs Make the Church More Concerned with "Doing" than "Being."

I (Gene) had a counselor remind me once that people are human *beings*, not human *doings*. Our worth is in who we *are* in Christ, not what we *do* for Him. The same holds true for churches. But like children who try to gain praise from their parents with "good works," churches and church leadership spend countless hours planning and coordinating the ongoing programs and events that fill church calendars. Bible studies, discipleship opportunities, music programs, seasonal "special" programs, meetings, and services become central to our worth. However, no matter how much each of the ongoing programs and special events are good in essence, a metamorphosis often takes place that transforms them from good, into bad, into ugly intrusions into a healthy, mission-focused life.

The Bible warns us that we can *do* things until we gain the whole world and still lose our hearts, and still not see hearts transformed nor lives changed (Mk. 8:36). Many members of our churches will hear Jesus say, "Depart from me" (Mt. 7:23) because they banked on doing good works for Him instead of being His "*Abba* child." Doing could possibly be one of the most deadly actions a local church imposes on its people. If doing is primary to a church's success, its members soon figure out that that must be what they are supposed to do. The church itself creates the perception that "more is better," doing is more important than being.

Take a hard look at your church's weekly schedule of activities, programs, and ministries. Sometimes it seems as if church activities barely leave time available in the typical week for a church family to eat a dinner at home. Add to the "church schedule" a family's nonchurch activities, and no wonder many churched families are so busy they are almost in a crisis mode. Instead of assisting people to have full and meaningful lives, we unknowingly insist people have full and exhausted lives. "The solution to our problem of crowded loneliness," according to Frazee, "involves a restructuring of our relationships and our time."[8]

Our addiction to doing also leads us to taking on more than is manageable. This not only affects church members but the church as a whole. We feel that the more we do, the more we feel we must do, and on and on it goes. The product we produce from our activities is far from God honoring. Giving His ministry just "a lick and a promise" can amount to dishonoring God. We agree with Sue Miller and David Stall, who confess, "[We] must choose to say yes to a reasonable workload that honors God, and no more."[9]

People far from God, the focus of CBSE, are not looking for more to do. Their PDAs, iPhones, and full calendar of activities are similar to the ones of those trying to help them trust Jesus. Their lives, too, are full, crammed with activities. They wonder, "How in the world am I going to successfully juggle everything already on my calendar?" They are not standing in line desiring something to do or attend, especially with "organized religion." Those far from God wonder if we are a "bit off center" because of the countless hours we devote to programs at our church.

How can we once again leverage programs to assist us in being the church? First, begin a systematic evaluation of each and every program. Ask these questions: What is the program's vision? How does it help complete the overall vision of the church? Is the program's vision being fulfilled? If not, why? Is there a better method to accomplish its vision? How is it unlike what is presently happening? What adjustments need to be made?

Second, ask each program's leadership how they might better assist people with the concept of being. Are their actions a by-product of who they are, or is who they are a result of what they do? Be careful not to create a "to do" list for them. Remain laser-focused on helping them determine who they are in Christ first and what they do as result of whose they are.

Third, regularly evaluate the spiritual development of members and regular attenders. (We will offer specific tools for doing this in an appendix online at www.chalicepress.com.) What tangible evidence is there that their involvement in your ministry has assisted the individual in becoming a more devoted follower of Christ? We are not number counting here. We are taking the time to seriously consider if what we are doing is producing quantifiable results toward our stated reason for being, the two Great C's.

Finally, allow people to share personal stories of their spiritual journeys as devoted followers of Christ. Help them to craft their stories to emphasize that doing comes after being. Yes, doing can play a major role in assisting people to being. However, spiritual transformation is our bottom line, not behavior modification.

2. Programs Take the Focus Off People and Their Needs.

The second way in which programs affect our time needed to become community-focused is that they take the focus off people and their needs. Along with God, Jesus, the Holy Spirit, and God's Word, only people will live for eternity. People are at the heart of the church's mission. People's lives hang in the balance, not church programs. But church always seems to put the focus on staffing programs, raising money for budgets and buildings, and making sure the organizational chart is filled—not on meeting the needs of people.

We are convinced that God will provide adequate leadership for a local church to operate at optimum performance, so that a church does not have to worry about if it will have enough leaders for the new church ministry year. However, many programmed-focused churches misplace the God-given resource of spiritually gifted leaders on maintenance rather than on mission. Programs become leadership leeches and suck the life-giving blood of church leadership from the body's veins.

Church programs cloud a church's vision. Churches can become so internally focused on their organizational needs that their existence and growth replaces the God-given vision for the church. It is hard enough to keep a church focused on the vision of reaching people, let alone an additional five, to ten, or even twenty programs, ministries, and events that demand constant attention. Focus is difficult to maintain. Nehemiah had to remind the people of the reason they risked their lives to rebuild the wall in order to return their attention to the task as their enemies attempted to draw their attention from their work. And his vision from God only took him fifty-two days to accomplish! (Neh. 6:15). We are attempting to build God-honoring churches that will stand the test of time. The apostle Paul warns us about the importance of staying focused in his letter to the church at Philippi (Phil. 3:14). He knew that focus was a critical issue for churches. Many things attempt to hijack or dilute the focus—even good, godly people.

3. Many Programs Do Not Match the Church's Culture.

Most existing churches have programs, ministries, and events in their weekly, monthly, or yearly calendar that have been around for years or decades. Many of those were started not because the program, ministry, or event was a good idea, or something that the church leadership felt was something that God was leading them to do. Many of those were started because some other church across town was doing it, or the denomination strongly suggested it. One of the best, older examples in many existing churches across the U.S. is family life centers.

Here's how it worked. First Church develops a dynamic recreational ministry and determines that they should own their building instead of constantly renting schools and community facilities. They build a family life center, and the church develops a recreational ministry and continues to grow rapidly.

What is Second Church to do? They do not have anything but a co-ed softball team. But because First Church built a family life center and people came, they believe, "If we build it, the people will come to us, too." Second Church leadership will tell you that they will develop the recreational ministry after the building is up and full. They go in debt to build and deepen their commitment to salaries and to upkeep on the facilities. Then equipment costs skyrocket as they complete the plans. The focus gradually shifts from reaching people through a recreational ministry to "paying for the family life center." What started as "a proven way to reach more people" becomes an albatross of debt and upkeep for the members of the church.

Church programs offered by denominations should be more like moving through the line of your local cafeteria where you pick and choose what your church wants and what matches your taste. All the items offered by your denomination are not to be consumed, and all denominational programs are not to be embraced out of loyalty or because that program has worked in one or two successful churches. Only a selected few match your church.

Before beginning a new program, a church must take time to adjust its culture to enable the program to be successful. For example, churches usually add programs without considering first which programs, ministry, or recurring events may have run their course and need to be eliminated. One of the local Baptist churches I (Steve) work with was running 300 in weekly attendance. They proudly had members serving in over 100 programs, ministries and church-wide events! You can only imagine the maintenance strain on that church's population. We acknowledge that new programs, ministries, and events need to be added from time to time. Everyone realizes the world is changing. However, by only adding and never reevaluating and even cutting programs, churches are committing a leadership crime.

Church works best when it is kept simple. The "Simple Church" movement has demonstrated that simple is better than complex when it comes to making disciples. Thom Rainer and Eric Geiger have concluded from their observations: "Churches with a simple process for reaching and maturing people are expanding the kingdom. Church leaders who have designed a simple biblical process to make disciples are effectively advancing the movement of the gospel. Simple churches are making a big impact."[10]

When leaders reduce complex program matrices to the essential processes of making disciples, these processes will fit the local church's culture better than imported programs from other churches and/or the denomination.

What we do must match who we are and what God is directing us to do. Not every church can be best at everything.

4. Programs Make It Easy to Put Faith in Our Efforts Instead of in God.

One of the constant struggles in church leadership is to depend on God for growing the church. We know you can build your church without God. Enough proven organizational and leadership models pragmatically work so that you really do not need God to grow your church. This may sound tongue-in-cheek or hyper-spiritual, but we know it to be true. Church leaders tend to default to attempt only what looks good on paper or what they know they can accomplish. They can control and manage programs, ministries, and events. They can hold paid staff accountable to keep the programs running. If the staff member doesn't meet expectations, then a leader encourages that person to leave to be replaced with someone who can.

We are frightened by how much churches do without relying on God. Given good planning with enough leadership, and churches believe they can make things happen with or without God. Programs give us a tangible gauge on how we are doing, but the work of changed hearts is different than the work of making widgets.

What are some indications your church may be more reliant on your church programs than on God?

- If you copy last year's calendar directly over to this year's calendar.
- If your attendance continues to decrease, volunteers are next to impossible to enlist, and yet the program, ministry, or event continues anyway.
- If your church budget has zero monies allocated for evaluation, research, and development.

- If your staff members fill their weekly schedules with program, ministry, and event maintenance rather than meeting the needs of people in the community directly or mobilizing people to do so.
- If you and your staff members look at every new guest that enters your buildings or small groups as a potential worker in their area of ministry.
- If you go through the entire church roster every year looking for volunteers to populate your programs, ministries, and events.
- If the first five points of church staff members' job descriptions pertain to maintenance or growth of existing church programs.

This is not an exhaustive list, but hopefully will point out how easily dependence on programs instead of God can happen. God must be the Giver and Motivator of all we do if we are to accomplish His vision for our churches.

5. Programs Can Easily Become the Tail(s) That Wags the Dog.

We (Steve's family) have two standard poodles as a part of our family, Samson and Delilah. My wife spent an enormous amount of time training Samson to be a Delta Society Therapy Dog. She takes Samson along to school to work with her special education students. Her dog also accompanies her to nursing and assisted living homes to visit with the residents there. Samson also goes weekly to the public library to be a part of the library's pet read program. Samson is about as good as a dog can get.

Delilah is my dog. She is not a therapy dog; she is like her owner: a little on the undisciplined side. (I blame this on being a puppy—the dog, not me—though that excuse will not be good much longer.). My wife thinks Delilah is ADHD. Her tail is constantly wagging. Her body is constantly in motion. It would wear out a healthy child to keep up with her. Delilah is as close to perpetual motion as any living creature I have observed.

Ever since Delilah joined our family, my attention can never be totally focused on anything when I am at home. When I call Samson to come, he walks slowly over to me. I call Delilah and she is all legs and tongue as she runs full out to me. I am using this book as a personal confession to share with my readers that I am a total failure as a dog trainer. The Dog Whisperer I'm not. Basically, you could say Delilah has become the tail that wags our family.

Churches sadly are little different than that of the Pate household. In a few instances they start a program like Samson. It does exactly what it is supposed to accomplish. You can even teach the old dog new tricks, and it catches hold quickly and performs at a high level. These programs are there to serve people, not be served by the people.

But then we have Delilah-like programs. They tend to dominate churches. They never quit. They rule the roost. When they are around, which is always, they demand attention. Why, because everything is there for their pleasure and to fulfill their needs. No matter if God is leading the church to start something new, they run, jump, bark, and slobber their demands so all eyes are focused on them. To make matters even worse, churches are prone to having multiple Delilah ministries, not Samson ones!

This makes keeping the main thing the main thing next to impossible. Church programs require more paid staff, more money. Such programs lower the contribution of volunteers to "line" fillers in an organizational chart. Servants to the mission no longer exist. The only servants are those who must maintain what happens every week to service those who show up and give.

Additionally, these type of church programs, ministries, and events—along with the church staff required to run them—become financial drains to the church budget. The longer they exist, the more money and ministerial time is required to keep them afloat.

6. Church Programs Can Easily Give the Church a False Sense of Success.

A list composed of what determines success for a business and a local church will have a few similar points, but also should look dramatically different. Church programs tend to blur out the differences. The bottom line for a local church is people and where they are going to spend eternity. Additionally, are people living a full and abundant life (Jn. 10:10)? The business bottom line is customers, dollars, profit, and growth.

We contend that church programs can easily drive a church away from its bottom line reason for existence. One of the detrimental side effects of a program-, ministry-, and event-focused church is that it can create leadership confusion. Leaders begin pulling the church simultaneously in multiple different directions. Multiple bottom lines then tend to appear instead of: Are we fulfilling the Great Commandment and the Great Commission?

7. Programs Make It Difficult to Honor a Person's Spiritual Gifts and Passion.

Church programs, ministries, and events are volunteer intensive. Because every program requires a number of volunteers, all—regardless of their spiritual gifting and passion—have to roll up their sleeves and do their part. The vacancies that programs, ministries, and events have in their volunteer structures become more important than maturing and releasing the individuals to function as living members of the body. If church programs remained static, that would create one issue. But because they are ever attempting to expand, that creates a larger issue. Programs compete for volunteers, and "super-members" end up serving in multiple positions, while others wonder why they can't make a contribution to what the church is trying to do. Quality suffers when churches begin a program, ministry, or event simply because the current activities are not fulfilling their potential. Often this is due to tired, over-worked, well-meaning volunteers.

Let us give you an example of how this takes place in a local church today. A particular church has been a small-group-driven church since its beginning roughly fifteen years ago. A lack of interest by the previous pastor and multiple staff changes eventually led the adult small groups to evolve into prayer and share times. They did no Bible study together, joined in no service together, and had no accountability to help each other develop spiritually. The groups ate food together and shared a brief ten-minute prayer time. They spent the rest of the time talking about whatever. They liked it that way.

The church called a new pastor. He did not have a great deal of experience with adult small groups, but he quickly recognized a problem in the small group ministry. His first thought was to begin a discipleship program and strongly encourage the elders and key leaders to go through a twenty-six–week curriculum.

He began with thirty people in attendance in the program and was thrilled, but he also recognized that the care for members was not adequate. So he asked the elders to divide up the church membership and create an elder family ministry. Each elder ended up with between fourteen and sixteen families.

Today this church has three programs—small groups, discipleship, and elder care—because the adult small groups failed to fulfill their responsibility. This is sadly duplicated over and over throughout churches across America.

We do not only overcommit volunteers' time but also the time of those who participate. Churches miss out on God-initiated encounters because His church has too much going on and has settled for a sub-par quality for its programs, ministries, and events. We have both heard Sue Miller, former director of PromiseLand at Willow Creek Community Church, say, "It should be a sin to bore a kid at church."

Therefore, it should not surprise us each time a church has an hour, everyone tries to figure out what church program we need to add so every family member has something to do or somewhere to go. More often than not, we waste kids', teenagers', and adults' time by babysitting them at church.

Once again, the critical issue we desire you, the reader, to deal with is: How can you keep everything you have going today and still create a church who desires to experience the two Great C's? Churches, plain and simple, have gone through the cafeteria line and placed on their trays far more than their trays will hold, or that they can consume!

8. New Programs Can Create an Unstable Foundation for Church Leadership.

As a consultant with churches, I (Steve) have numerous opportunities to visit with key church leaders and volunteers. One of the statements I hear over and over from them is, "Why is it every time our pastor or church staff members attend a conference they come back and add or change what we are doing?" They are right, because we have both been there and done that.

How often do you go to your grocery store, see a new product, and, whether you need the product or not, it goes into your basket? Churches have become consumers of the new. Churches constantly add the newest packaged cereal or latest health product to their baskets, without ever taking anything out.

If any two people live for quality improvement, it is us. Both of us spend a great deal of every day trying to figure out how to make what we do better. Churches should constantly evaluate and make course corrections. However, constantly changing to new and different depreciates existing ministries. Members perceive that all the time and effort they spent on the last new thing was not worth the effort.

Any time church leaders add a new program, ministry, or event, they take the chance of invalidating proven programs. Local church leaders and volunteers do not really demand much. They enjoy serving in meaningful service arenas. They are the ones who carve out their precious hours to give to their Lord and His church. As church leaders who steward people's resources, we must keep the vision crystal clear. This demands we set a course direction and only adjust when it is absolutely clear a course correction is necessary. It also means we must not muddy things up by creating competing organizations, programs, ministries, and events that create confusion among those who have given their lives to the cause of Christ.

9. If a Program, Ministry, or Event Is to Be Removed, It Is Strongly Likely This Will Become a Point of Conflict.

The "good ole days" are three of the most dangerous words that can ever be said in a local church, replacing: "We have never done it that way!" Previous program, ministry, and event leadership too often become relics or untouchable saints. In the present, those programs, like Wednesday night fellowship meals and prayer circles, are fondly remembered like Camelot and the Knights of the Round Table. In actuality, the program had a minimal number attending weekly, and only a small, tenured group did all the cooking and serving. No one was added to the fellowship by all the effort. But, the memories are exaggerated in both numbers and results. So, when a leader offers an alternative to the stagnant, ineffective ministry, those involved resist any change because to them the current reality is everything the leader is offering them with the new concept.

Granted, many church programs, ministries, and events contributed to church growth. However, many have long past outlived their effectiveness. The lack of regularly evaluating these often presents the church with a crisis. A church will actually allow a program, ministry, or event to take them to the point of permanently closing their doors. The waste of Kingdom resources (money and volunteer hours) is atrocious.

Another key negative aspect that we much consider about out-0lived programs, ministries, and events is that they tend to keep too many eyes looking backward instead of forward. Many churches have absolutely no difficulty in looking backward; it's forward thinking they tend to lack. Programs, ministries, and events become so interweaved into the local church that they become the "end" instead of a means to the end.

10. Perpetuating Programs Squelches the Creativity of Volunteers.

Programs and ministries tend to be the offspring of denominational offices and agencies. The denomination often offers produced resources for these programs and ministries. The sale of these resources in turn gives us the next round of new programs and ministries and the next line of new resources for support.

The next part of the puzzle our denominations tend to develop is the seminar and conference notebook. Attend this or that conference, and you will leave with a detailed step-by-step implementation process. We can still remember hearing our denominational leaders say, "And we've got everything in these materials you will ever need. It is outlined and as easy as one, two, three." Where is the local church to add its creativity? Where and how can a local congregation make it their own if they are to do things "by the book"?

George Barna, at conferences at both Glorieta and Ridgecrest Conference Centers in the summer of 2004, shared his recent research indicating a direct correlation between a church writing its own curriculum and materials and the church prevailing. We acknowledge that simply writing curriculum is not the "missing link," but writing your own materials naturally causes several changes. Intentionality becomes crucial. Direction becomes critical. Communication between church departments operates at a higher level. Additionally, a team atmosphere is much easier to create.

As a part of our ongoing attempt to empower and strengthen our churches, we (Denton Baptist Association) have begun offering writing seminars. These seminars are designed to improve the writing abilities of those already responsible with their church's curriculum development and creation. We believe organic development of programs, ministries, events, and the materials to support them are effective when a local church realizes the potential creativity and resources within its own membership.

The CBSE philosophy or methodology of ministry provides churches with the possibility of *increasing* the average number of hours members are willing to contribute to fulfilling the Great Commandment and the Great Commission. When serving in their "sweet spot" of spiritual gifting and passion, members do not seem to tire as quickly, and are able to remain positive in difficult situations and produce fruit.

Churches should present to the elders, leadership team, and/or deacons budgets that contain not only how monies will be dispersed, but also detailed budget of person-hours and how they will be invested to further the Kingdom. Both are important. Both must be allocated according to the Holy Spirit's guidance. Only by considering the interrelatedness of money and person-hours will a church really understand how it allocates its resources.

The Barrier of Underdeveloped Passion and Spiritual Gifts

Jesus' departing words prior to His ascension told of the coming of the Holy Spirit: "But you will receive power when the Holy Spirit has come upon you" (Acts 1:8a). However, Jesus did not stop there. He went on to tell His followers why the Holy Spirit was coming. He said, "And you shall be My witnesses both in Jerusalem, and in all Judea and Samaria, and even to the remotest part of the earth" (Acts 1:8b).

The Bible teaches that the Holy Spirit gives Christ-followers special abilities to fulfill the Great Commission. "But one and the same Spirit works all these things, distributing to each one individually just as He wills" (1 Cor. 12:11). The Holy Spirit distributes gifts for a specific purpose. "But to each one is given the manifestation of the Spirit for the common good" (1 Cor. 12:7). Bruce Bugbee ties together both verses when he writes, "Spiritual gifts are divine endowments. They are used for spiritual purposes. They are abilities God has given us to make our unique contribution."[11] Spiritual gifts answer the question, "What do I do when I serve Christ?"

The Bible lists specific spiritual gifts: "And He gave some as apostles, and some as prophets, and some as evangelists, and some as pastors and teachers, for the equipping of the saints for the work of service, to the building up of the body of Christ" (Eph. 4:11–12). Other spiritual gifts can be found in the following passages: 1 Corinthians 12:8–10; 1 Corinthians 12:28; Romans 12:6–8; 1 Peter 4:9; Exodus 31:3–5; Romans 8:2–27; and Psalm 150. However, many differing interpretations of each of the passages produce a difference of opinion among Christ-followers as to whether each gift listed is indeed a "spiritual gift." (*Network* lists the following spiritual gifts and their supporting scripture references: wisdom, knowledge, faith, healing, miracles, prophecy, discernment, tongues, interpretation, apostleship, teaching, helps, administration, encouragement, giving, leadership, mercy, evangelism, shepherding, hospitality, craftsmanship, creative communication, and intercession.[12])

Regardless of what we consider a complete list of spiritual gifts, a Christ-follower's passion and spiritual gifts play an important role in finding a fruitful place of service in the mission of the church. Passion is God-given, and addresses the "where" question of ministry. Wayne Cordeiro, pastor of New Hope Community Church in Honolulu, has observed:

> God has equipped us to serve through the use of our gifts, and if we are unaware of them, our ability to serve Him will be immensely impeded. God knew beforehand that His plan could never be accomplished by an act of human will. It could only be accomplished through the strength He supplied in the form of spiritual gifts.[13]

The *Network* description is, "Passion is the God-given desire that compels us to make a difference in a particular ministry."[14] Passion helps the Christ-follower to know where he is to serve. It gives the Christ-follower direction, energy, and motivation to serve in a particular place. That a Christ-follower feels more deeply about one thing than do others is by God's design. The promise of the ancients is, "Trust in the LORD and do good; / Dwell in the land and cultivate faithfulness. / Delight yourself in the LORD; / And He will give you the desires of your heart. / Commit your way to the LORD, / Trust also in Him, and He will do it" (Ps. 37:3–5). The apostle Paul's personal confession was, "But when God, who had set me apart even from my mother's womb and called me through His grace, was pleased to reveal His Son in me so that I might preach Him among the Gentiles, I did not immediately consult with flesh and blood" (Gal. 1:15–16).

The combination of spiritual gifts and passion in the life of a Christ-follower guides him to the unique role that he can play in the body of Christ. Paul taught the church in Corinth, "But now God has placed the members, each one of them, in the body, just as He desired" (1 Cor. 12:18). God arranged the parts of the body exactly how He wanted them. The individual Christ-follower's unique role as an eye, hand, or foot is critical if the body is to function properly (Rom. 12:5).

We believe that churches cannot reach their potential when those joined to the mission and vision of the church either (1) do not know their God-given passion and spiritual gift(s) or (2) if those aspects of who they are in Christ are underdeveloped. We have observed that those who work out of their Spirit-empowered passion and gifts rarely burn out, and instead attract others to their ministry. Conversely, we have already noted that those who serve the institution rather than live out of their passion become discontent and often move from ministry to ministry, seeking their "sweet spot," or quit altogether out of frustration.

Part of spiritual maturity is to know and to nurture these parts of who we are in Christ. One way to mobilize your people is to lead them through such a discovery process. I (Gene) have done this in my church through my workbook, *Jesus on Leadership*.[15] Each member develops her S.E.R.V.E. profile, which helps her discover and connect her *s*piritual gifts, *e*xperiences, *r*elational styles, *v*ocational skills, and *e*nthusiasm (or, passion) to ministry opportunities within the church organization and in the mission field of the church. People are more likely to step up to serve when church leadership guides them in the discovery of these items and leads them to places where they can live them out with a connection to the church's mission and vision.

The Barrier of Church Structure and Control

Prior to the section that describes the foundations for CBSE, we want to point out how policies, organizational structure, and church programs tend to protect themselves when a new focus or ministry such as CBSE infringes on their turf. Bill Easum called "control" the sacred cow in churches almost a decade ago when he wrote *Sacred Cows Make Gourmet Burgers.*[16] "Control" is how you protect existing processes and ministries. Control raises its ugly head so often we have grown to expect it when we consult or coach church leaders in change.

Control finds its foothold in expressions of church structure. Controlling members tend to use church constitutions and bylaws to maintain the status quo rather than produce freedom among the members. A lack of trust produces written policies and procedures for everything we can imagine. Frightened or hurt members write many policies as the result of prior issues within the church. The church faces an issue and tries to do everything possible to prevent that particular issue from coming up again. The barriers to creating a permission-giving leadership structure are so numerous that when we attempt to change the old structure we know the results will be less than optimal. Control is often so strong that to step outside the "box" even to preserve the church's existence is refused. Try to update a constitution or building use policy that has been around for some time, and you will know what we are talking about.

Businesses and corporations can address issues and make sweeping changes rapidly. For churches, you and I know it is a different story. We tell church leadership that churches live in "half speed" of that of business. Staff-led churches can run most like businesses, but to affect any changes elder-led churches that include volunteers must wait for the once-a-week members to catch up. To make the changes necessary to have a community-based ministry, church leaders and staff must trust their members and the Holy Spirit's leadership in their lives.

An example of the fear of loss of control is that some churches have opposed small groups meeting off campus because of the "what happen ifs." For example, What happens if

- the small group leader interprets a passage in an unacceptable manner?
- the small group studies curriculum other than what is provided?
- the small group follows heretical teaching?
- the small group talks negatively about our church?

Churches have fooled themselves into thinking that because Sunday school classes meet "on campus," none of these things can take place and everything is "under control." But I (Steve) can personally share with you many situations where every one of the "ifs" listed above have taken place in adult Sunday school classes. The bottom line is, small groups, adult Sunday school classes, and people serving in the community as salt and light are only as effective as the leadership leading them. Leadership that releases other leaders, not controlling leadership, is what is so badly needed in our local churches today.

Jesus has given His bride, the church, the global responsibility of living out the Great Commandment and the Great Commission. Quite possibly the most often quoted passage pertaining to the local church today is Acts 2:42–47. The passage provides a description of the attitudes, behaviors, and actions of the first Christ-followers who sought to be the church as Christ commissioned them to be. Here it is:

> They were continually devoting themselves to the apostles' teaching and to fellowship, to the breaking of bread and to prayer. Everyone kept feeling a sense of awe; and many wonders and signs were taking place through the apostles. And all those who had believed were together and had all things in common; and they began selling their property and possessions, and were sharing them with all as anyone might have need. Day by day continuing with one mind in the temple, and breaking bread from house to house, they were taking their meals together with gladness and sincerity of heart, praising God and having favor with all the people. And the Lord was adding to their number day by day those who were being saved.

This description of the early church's actions in the community and with themselves is the basis for CBSE, which is the church *in service* to the needs of others. I (Gene) have previously observed that although Jesus "dressed like a servant and acted like a slave, he still led."[17] Christ-followers and churches must clearly understand their biblical role and make it become the reason for their actions.

Foundation Summary

Christ-followers *must* engage their world. Bill Hybels says, "This means that in a very real way the future of the world rests in the hands of local congregations like yours and mine. It's the church or its lights out."[18] God has but one plan: from God, through us (2 Cor. 5). "The local church is the hope of the world and its future rests primarily in the hands of its leaders."[19] The local church must find new ways to engage and serve people in their communities.

A community-engaged church finds opportunities that were not visible until the members left the "walls" of their buildings and member groups and entered the needs of those around them in the name of Jesus. Erwin McManus wrote:

When the church is a movement, it becomes a place of refuge for an unbelieving world. The church becomes the place where the seekers finally find the God they were searching for. The church becomes the place for the broken and the weary to finally find the healing and the help they've cried for. The church becomes the place where the lonely and outcast are finally embraced and loved in the community of Christ.[20]

When the church as described in Acts 2 becomes engaged, it becomes the place of transformation. Jesus did not call out the church to minister to just those on the "inside." The last sentence in the Gospel of Matthew is, "And lo, I am with you always, even to the end of the age" (Mt. 28:20b). God is building His church, and we are His instruments. There is nothing capable of stopping the local church. Jesus said, "Upon this rock I will build My church; and the gates of Hades will not overpower it" (Mt. 16:18). The church is an "unstoppable force," against which even the "gates of Hades" cannot prevail. We confess with John Ortberg, "I believe a fitting description for the church would be this: a community of people who present living proof of a loving God to a watching world."[21] To activate this image of the church, churches must assist their members to find their place of service for the Kingdom in the community. If we hope to see the Great Commission fulfilled, we must engage our communities in servant evangelism with Christ, our Rescuer and Leader, as our example and motivation. Ortberg concluded, "Jesus did not come as a servant in spite of the fact that He is God; He came precisely because of the fact He is God.[22]

QUESTIONS FOR CONSIDERATION

1. Return to the formula on page 25 (AWA x ATpPpWK = TPH available). Are you investing your church's Total Person-Hours in Great Commandment endeavors?

2. Which of the "Church Program Barriers" do you personally suffer with the most? What next steps do "you/the church" need to take to overcome the "program" issue(s)?

3. What church structure and control issues is your church currently facing? What steps might you take to address and overcome this barrier?

4. Is your church a non-serving church? Generally, does your church serve its members or the community better? What is the current

ratio? Is that ratio acceptable to you? What next steps might you take to address this issue?

5. Does your church have a clearly defined picture of what a devoted follower of Christ is?

Notes

[1]Randy Frazee, *Making Room for Life* (Grand Rapids: Zondervan, 2003).

[2]For more information, go to www.dallasprovidencehomes.org or contact them by mail at Dallas Providence Homes, Inc., PO Box 866903, Plano, TX 75086.

[3]Ray Oldenburg, *The Great Good Place: Cafes, Coffee Shops, Bookstores, Bars, Hair Salons and Other Hangouts at the Heart of a Community* (New York: Marlowe and Company, 1999), 287.

[4]Ken Blanchard, *The One Minute Manager Balances Work and Life* (New York: Quill, 1986), 13.

[5]www.davidzach.com

[6]Richard Swenson, *Margin* (Colorado Springs: NavPress, 1992), 149.

[7]Stephen R. Covey, *The Seven Habits of Highly Effective People* (New York: Simon and Schuster, 1989), 149.

[8]Frazee, *Making Room for Life,* 37.

[9]Sue Miller and David Stall, *Making Your Children's Ministry the Best Hour of Every Kid's Week* (Grand Rapids: Zondervan, 2004), 141.

[10]Thom Rainer and Eric Geiger, *Simple Church* (Nashville: B&H Publishers, 2006), 14.

[11]Bruce Bugbee, Don Cousins, and Bill Hybels, *Network Leader's Guide* (Grand Rapids: Zondervan, 1994), 78.

[12]Ibid., 114–20.

[13]Wayne Cordeiro, *Doing Church as a Team* (Honolulu: New Hope Publishing, 1998), 53.

[14]Bugbee, Cousins, and Hybels, *Network,* 56.

[15]C. Gene Wilkes, *Jesus on Leadership* (Wheaton, Ill.: Tyndale House, 1998).

[16]William M. Easum, *Sacred Cows Make Gourmet Burgers* (Nashville: Abingdon Press, 1995).

[17]Wilkes, *Jesus on Leadership.*

[18]Bill Hybels, *Courageous Leadership* (Grand Rapids: Zondervan, 2002), 21–22.

[19]Ibid., 27.

[20]Erwin Raphael McManus, *An Unstoppable Force* (Loveland: Group, 2001), 65.

[21]Quoted in Robert Lewis and Rob Wilkins, *The Church of Irresistible Influence* (Grand Rapids: Zondervan, 2001), 41.

[22]John Ortberg, *The Life You've Always Wanted* (Grand Rapids: Zondervan, 1997), 106.

3

Place

Why the Local Church Must Understand This Principle

Twelve years ago, I (Steve) accepted the consultant position with the Denton Baptist Association in Texas. My wife and I had to decide for the first time in our adult lives which church we would join and serve with. Looking for a church that had a dynamic children's and students' program along with our preferred style of service helped us to narrow the list. Each family member looked for something different. My wife, because she was passionate about children and an effective children's ministry, focused on that particular aspect of church life. My teenage daughter wanted a large, active student ministry, with a lot of good-looking guys, of course. My youngest daughter loves music and the arts. She could care less about other aspects of church life. I found myself looking at the church's list of this week's programs, ministries, and events. For the first time, I would have to add church activities to my already busy calendar. As a staff member, those activities were part of my "job," and I found space for them in my workday schedule. "The list" became one of my determining factors in my choice of a church home.

If you have been a pastor or church staff member, you can relate to our first eighteen years as a family. Our personal and family calendars revolved around the church's calendar. For you who are college and seminary students anxiously anticipating church ministry and service, beware. For you who are church volunteers and have felt the stress of juggling those responsibilities in addition to a forty-plus-hour work week, family, community and civic organizations, and school activities, I empathize. I now know the struggle ministers such as Gene and I create for your lives.

Gene and I have both heard from volunteers in our churches, "Don't you understand we have a life outside the church!" To be honest, neither of us did. We insisted that folks love God, love others, and love their local church. All that love was to take place in their homes and church. After weekly chiding from the pulpit, we expected that good Christians would reply, "Sign me up! Just tell me when and where!" when we asked them to join us on a project.

I (Steve) cannot speak for my family, but, while we were looking, whenever a smiling usher at a church handed me the Sunday program/ bulletin I found myself immediately looking for the church calendar. I often had it memorized before taking two or three steps into the auditorium. I would whisper to myself, "Too much on the calendar, too many opportunities for service, ministry, and spiritual development." My vote was no. I could not add that much to my crammed calendar of activities.

I then began to look for one or two things that appeared most important to the church, but I never found anything that said, "This is the most important thing we do. Help us." Every program, event, or service opportunity seemed to carry the same level of importance. Someone would always "plug" one or two programs or events during the announcement time in the service. Those became the "needs de jour" to me, and it appeared anyone and everyone was invited to participate. What about an experienced practitioner like me? Was there any place the church could leverage my talents, passions, and spiritual gifts? I wanted to stand up and scream, "Don't you understand we have a life outside the church! I don't have time for all this stuff! You are going to kill me!"

I secretly hoped someone from one of the churches with a jammed weekly schedule would ask me about joining their church. I was prepared with a ten-minute, no-holds-barred, tongue-lashing. All I needed was a candidate. Then frustration set in. No one would ask me to join! I guess they read the frustration in my eyes, or they did not know what to do with me if I joined. No one ever stepped forward offering themselves up as sacrificial lamb.

Like Every Other Church Out There

My family finally joined a mission church to help in any way we could. This ranged from accepting a leadership position to changing baby diapers. We thought this would be a good move for us, because the church had very little in the way of church events and programming. Some of that had to do with renting facilities for their weekly services, but a great deal had to do with the ministry philosophy of the pastor.

At this writing, we have been members for nearly three years. The church has bought land, built a building, more than tripled in weekly attendance, and has a weekly church calendar that would kill a healthy young adult. Soon I had a conversation with our pastor regarding a proposal to offer four weekend services. The conversation provided me the platform to tell him, "We've done it. We now look like every other church out there. We have a weekly schedule so full that you have no idea of all the weekly events and programs that happen each week. We've ceased being a movement and have become a church!" Of course, any red-blooded, American pastor of such a church would be proud, not sad, after that sort of statement. His church had grown so big he did not know everything that was going on! However, my purpose was not to compliment him, but to invite him to consider the problem we had created for our people.

So how did we get there? Initially, this was the last thing we wanted. We had fallen out of being part of a movement and had adopted a local church mentality. We were no longer mission-field focused and had missed Doug Pagitt and Tony Jones' injunction, "If Christ-followers seek a kingdomlike life both in their church community and within the surrounding culture, they must operate as a movement that follows God's mission to the world."[1]

We planned to do preschool and children's ministry, worship, small groups, and to intentionally involve members in community and civic organizations as "salt and light." That was all, nothing else. Now, almost every day of the week and every part of the day, we have meetings and activities. I believe an inherent change takes place in people's thinking when they engage a church with this much activity. They somehow become convinced that the more events, programs, and ministries, the more like a New Testament church they are. But, is our church really more like an Acts 2 church now than we were nearly three years ago?

Churches scream for people's time along with every other organization, business, and school. Many families cannot sit down and enjoy a meal together because of all they have committed to do. At best they share meals on the run. All soliciting organizations think their activities are the most important and that I have the time to help them. They want me to make their activity number one or at least number two in my life priorities. A place on my calendar has become more and more difficult to find. Sadly, the church only adds to the problem.

Place and Its Meaning for All of Us

The word *place* signifies something different in our culture than most of us would expect. Place to us (the authors) is a prioritized period of time which an individual is forced, feels obligated, or chooses to invest who they are. For example, if you are anything like us, when the in-laws hold family reunions, we are much more likely to feel *obligated* to attend than we feel like *choosing* to attend. Granted, the perspective we take regarding a reunion depends upon our spouses. We would seldom initiate a discussion about the family gatherings. They are not in our top three "places" in life. We do not place family reunions in our priorities. Let us explain it this way.

Several years ago while attending a leadership conference, I (Steve) heard a conference speaker explain the vision and strategy of Starbucks, one of the most successful companies in the U.S. today. The leadership's vision was simple and clear: to have a coffee shop on every street corner, which has been adjusted at the writing of this book to meet more realistic goals. When Gene traveled to central China in 2006, he found three Starbucks already in a city probably not on even the most seasoned traveler's list of "cities in China with a Starbucks." The branded coffee shops are so numerous in the community around Gene's home that some staff and members refer to the area Starbucks franchises as "Legacy East," "Legacy South," and "Legacy West," respectively.

The speaker said the strategy is a two-pronged approach. The first is to build Starbucks Coffee Shops. We affirm they are doing an excellent job in fulfilling this part of their vision. The second emphasis is for their loyal customers to buy their product and brew it in their home. The company expects these customers to invite their neighbors and friends to share the brewing experience. As the discussion continued, the conference leader went on to say Starbucks understands that people have very few "places" available to them today. *The first two "places" people have are either home and work, or work and home. The battle is over third place. Starbucks has said they want to be third place in the U.S.* This is a part of the company's goals.

Questions jumped to my mind as I listened and made my way back to my room: "What place is the local church for most people?" What place should it be? First, second, third, or farther down the list? Does the Bible contain direction concerning "place"? As the local church goes after first, second, or third place, with whom will they do battle? Why haven't church leaders understood that they are in a battle for a "place" in people's lives? Why do churches add places instead of leveraging the places that are already central to people's lives? Why do so many churches want their members to prioritize the church as a place ahead of a member's family and work? Why do local churches lag years behind the corporate world in understanding the importance of "place"?

We acknowledge that the corporate world strives for greater returns and profits, things the Bible makes perfectly clear will not last. However, businesses encourage their employees to serve in community and civic organizations. For example, we know of businesses that have adopted a neighborhood and who ask their employees to volunteer time and money to build a playground for the area children. Corporations know this investment generates goodwill in the community and is a way they can "give back" to those who share the same neighborhood as they do. Businesses understand the importance of employees strategically "placed" in the community.

The church exists to love God and *all* people–including people in the community who are far from God. We know the Bible teaches that the things of this world will not stand the test of time. While the investments a business makes in the community may temporarily improve the lives of people there, the Bible teaches those improvements will not stand the test of time. The church, on the other hand, is in the business of changed lives for eternal purposes. So, why isn't the local church leading out in "community service" strategy? Why isn't it asking its members either to create a "place" to serve people in their community or to help members see that their current service in the community is really a place of ministry? Why are churches standing back and allowing for-profit business to do what the Bible calls the church to do as salt and light? Don't we really believe people's lives are hanging in the balance and that everyone will spend eternity somewhere? Ray Oldenburg's seminal work, *The Great Good Place: Cafes, Coffee Shops, Bookstores, Bars, Hair Salons and Other Hangouts at the Heart of a Community,* provides insight into the concept or principle of place. When we read this book, our hearts began to beat faster for churches to understand the battle for place. Churches don't understand the landscape. We don't know the players. To be honest, we do not even know we are in a battle, let alone know we are losing it.

We believe for most American church members the church is not first, second, third, or even fourth place in their lives. And you don't have to be a statistical genius to figure where those far from God place the organized church's activities on their priority lists. For families in both groups, after family and work, third and fourth places generally belong to school activities and personal or family interests. Little league, children's lessons (dance, karate, voice, art, piano, etc.), recreational activities (skiing, golf, boating, hunting, fishing, etc.), leisure activities, school activities, and community and civic organization activities take up so much time there is apparently no "place" for anything else to fit.

What is the appropriate number of places an individual should maintain in his or her life? Is it three (home, work, and church)? Is it four, five, or more? What would you describe as the number of places that fit into a fully devoted follower of Christ's lifestyle?

To grasp the stress our culture is under regarding "place," let me encourage you to return your thoughts to chapter 2 and the formula to calculate the number of volunteer hours it takes to sustain your ministries. If you have not completed the formula, please do so now.

Weekly Average Attendance _____ X

The Average Amount of Time Each Person in Attendance Gives the Church Each Week, Including: Worship, Bible study and all meetings _____

= Total Person-Hours Available to "Run" the Church

_____.

Whether we as ministers and church leaders like it or not, members do not have an infinite amount of hours per week they will give their church. If we continue to push members to give more and more, then when will they have time to develop relationships with individuals far from God? When will they have time to be "salt and light" in their community? Can you see why the church will continue to be seen by the community as less and less important?

So what can possibly be the solution?

Why can't the church support its members when they are involved in their third, fourth, and fifth place activities? Why can't the local church encourage members to serve in secular and civic organizations instead of only serving church programs? Are we really going to increase the numerical size of heaven by adding additional church programs and enlisting volunteers to serve these programs?

In those other places, members have the possibility for connection to people far from God who share similar interests. In those places,

Christ-followers have the opportunity to be salt and light. The church must begin to assist people with understanding their passion and spiritual gifts and encourage them to be salt and light in the other places in their lives.

Now I realize churches have far too often gotten a new idea and implemented the idea before doing all of the critical thinking and planning. So just allowing members to serve in secular and civic organizations will not accomplish the big vision. Members are to be trained in ways to effectively share their faith. Additionally, members need to have a working knowledge on how to develop relationships. Leveraging the individual's felt needs, CBSE has the strong possibility of changing the current trajectory of the church in America.

This leads to a foundational question: Are we to build the church through programs and events, or are we to be a biblically functioning community through our engagement in the broader community? It is a discussion and an ultimate decision that must be made. People just do not have time for everything.

Yes, the battle for places *is* critical for the church to understand. It is urgent for those who are Christ-followers. Determining "place" allows the church to become much more effective in developing Christ-followers into fully devoted followers. However, it is *critical* for those who are far from God. We are asking people to add a "place" to their already busy lives. The local church has the responsibility to ensure that, when someone adds church to their personal "place" list, it must make a difference for them, the community, and the world!

With all the negative publicity connected to many local churches, we must realize we are often asking people to add something that has little or no preconceived positive potential for their lives. To be honest, church is generally not on their radar screens and may be the last thing they want to add. (A suggested process to assist your church to deal with the "place" issue is provided later in chapter 6.)

However, the local church must seriously consider "place" and provide margin in its members' lives for other reasons. Oldenburg stated, "Community social life is necessary to have a healthy religious life, and if the church is going to succeed it must recognize the social needs of the community and assume its share of the leadership in social activities."[2] These are indeed strategic words for the church. The local church must be connected into the very fabric of the community's DNA if it is to effectively engage people far from God. It cannot distance itself from the community it is in and disconnect from the very people it is to reach.

Additionally, the local church must reengage in the culture and give solid credible reasons for the church's existence. Far too many people see no value in the local church. We are losing a public relations battle far too many of us are not even aware we are in.

The church must become involved with assisting its members with the third, forth, fifth place battle(s). With the fast-paced life we live, it is only in third, forth, or fifth places that we can find relaxation and the true meaning in life. Ray Oldenburg states, "Third place friendships, first of all, complement more intimate relations. Those who study human loneliness generally agree that the individual needs intimate relationships and that he or she also needs affiliation."[3] The local church should begin seeing its role as being God's equipping center for accomplishing this responsibility.

God understood from the beginning how important relationships are for His creation. After noticing Adam alone, God made Eve because, as the Bible says, "It is not good for the man to be alone; I will make him a helper suitable for him" (Gen. 2:18). Oldenburg states, "We are, after all, social animals. We are an associating species whose nature is to share space just as we share experiences; few hermits are produced in any human culture. A habitat that discourages association, one in which people withdraw to privacy as turtles into their shells, denies community and leaves people lonely in the midst of many."[4] My fear is many churches have actually encouraged disassociation and have become turtles in their own shells, denying that people are lonely and desperate for someone to make room in their third place for them.

In *The Great Good Place* are the following haunting words:

> In recent years the psychiatric profession has detected a substantial jump in the incidence of depression among children, an intriguing finding in that children have always seemed immune from depression. But was it children immune, or was it childhood? When kids were free to wander around their neighborhoods, to follow their own interests, to be creative in their own fashion, and to match activities to their own moods rather than to adult-imposed schedules, the antidotes to depression may well have been built into the structure of childhood fears. Today, youngsters find little release from the fetish imposed upon them. As their young lives are continually warped and molded to fit schedules based upon adult values and motivations, is it not to be expected that

they should manifest such adult reactions as depression and chronic boredom?[5]

It isn't enough we have messed up our own lives, but the social illness is being passed on to our children. It is not just the school, community, and civic organizations. The church must also accept and own its responsibility for the issues our society is facing and say, "Enough is enough." The local church must move from the problem side to the solution side of the equation.

The dilemmas our churches are facing are real. Churches still evaluate pastors and staff according to the number of church programs they have effectively up and running. Churches continue to evaluate pastors and staff by their ability to enlist individuals to serve in their ministry. Churches also continue to evaluate pastors and staff according to their ability to work within the existing structure.

We all know the current results we are experiencing are dismal. Therefore, we as church leaders must lead our churches in understanding that the old ways of evaluating pastor and staff performance are not as relevant as they were in the past. We must assist our churches in understanding the current affairs of our church and those in the community. We have always been taught the first responsibility of a leader in a business or a local church is to define reality.

"Place" is a critical principle for all church leaders to understand and apply possibly more critical than any of us would ever verbalize or consider. Everyone in your church has "placed" your church between "one" to "five" on his or her personal "place" list. If they are present, your church has a "place" in their lives. There is some value they have in your "place."

The one thing we cannot continue doing is operating in the same fashion we have in the past. Just because they currently have your church as one of their "places" does not mean they will tomorrow. It would be difficult to find a church that does not lose even one member each year because that (former) member has shifted down his or her priority list the "place" of the church.

The bottom line is, we have a life-changing message, a message that literally can change the trajectory of a person's life, yet no "place" to deliver it. The church must re-engage in its culture. It must allow members to place involvement in schools, community, and civic organizations at a higher "place" than that of the local church. "It is a fact of social life that the number, kind, and availability of friends depends upon where one may engage them."[6]

QUESTIONS FOR DISCUSSION

1. Currently the "places" in my life are:
2. I am forced to have these places in my life:
3. I am obligated to have these places in my life:
4. I have chosen to have these places in my life:
5. Am I following the biblical model?
6. What are the known "places" our members have chosen to invest their time?
7. What steps do we need to take to assist members and regular attenders with personal and congregational "place" issues?
8. What "place" in our community could I invest myself in and potentially be used by God to enlarge the numerical size of heaven?
9. What place(s) in my church do I feel forced or obligated to be in when I would choose rather to be in a place in the community where people are far from God?

Notes

[1]Doug Pagitt and Tony Jones, *An Emergent Manifesto of Hope* (Grand Rapids: Baker Books, 2007), 139.

[2]Ray Oldenburg, *The Great Good Place: Cafes, Coffee Shops, Bookstores, Bars, Hair Salons and Other Hangouts at the Heart of a Community* (New York: Marlowe and Company, 1999), 74.

[3]Ibid., 63.

[4]Ibid., 203.

[5]Ibid., 271.

[6]Ibid., 60.

4

Understanding
Community-Based
Servant Evangelism

To say that I (Steve) love sports would be an understatement. Football, baseball, hockey, basketball, soccer, golf, Indy car racing, skiing, track and field—you name it, and odds are I have spent hours either watching or playing the sport you name. Several years ago when I participated more than watched, I looked forward to time spent with friends who were also sports nuts and Christ-followers. We had a great deal in common—sports and faith. Conversations came easy.

When my son was five years old, he began playing soccer. He quickly made a friend, and before I knew it, they were constantly together. Living in the South, I assumed my son's new best friend and his family were Christians. I was wrong. The Wrights (not their real names) were great people who were loving, caring, compassionate, and would do anything to help someone in need. They loved their three children and were great parents. They instilled some Christian values and principles into their lives, even if they didn't call them Christian values. Therefore, I was glad that the Wrights' liked our son being best friends, too.

One Saturday afternoon the phone rang. The Wrights wanted my son to spend the night. They said I could pick him up after lunch on Sunday afternoon. As we packed, I sent "Sunday" clothing along, assuming they would go to church in the morning.

Sunday afternoon on the drive back home, I asked where his friend went to church that morning. My son replied, "Oh, we didn't go to church. We watched cartoons all morning. It was great, Dad!" I suddenly was embarrassed that I had never asked the family about the most important part of their lives: their relationship with Christ.

Over the next two years, my family and I developed a great relationship with the Wrights. We spent more time with them than we spent with our churched friends. Our love for the family grew to the point we could not stand the thought of them spending eternity separated from the Father. Larry, the father, loved playing softball, so we played together in a city league. A Vietnam vet, Larry had lost one of his legs stepping on a land mine. One of the best nights I ever had playing softball was when Larry dove for a ball hit down the third baseline. He missed the ball, which allowed two runs to score. When he stood up, his artificial leg had spun around 180 degrees with his toes facing backward. The opposing player standing on third base screamed, "Please sit down, it will be okay. We'll get the ambulance here as soon as possible." As the player ran toward the gas station to call (prior to cell phones) for help, Larry simply reached down and spun his leg around, slapped his glove and yelled, "Let's play ball!" Both teams were rolling on the ground laughing.

The ride home after the game was some of the best minutes we ever shared together. We laughed to the point of tears. It became a strategic night in our relationship, which led to him finally opening up his closed heart to seriously consider spiritual matters.

I continued to play softball with Larry, and soon found myself volunteering to be our sons' soccer coach. I invested many hours I felt I did not have in that team of boys and their parents. That extra time invested in practice and games, along with interaction with the Wrights and families like theirs, created trusting relationships that resulted in eternal differences in all of our lives.

Our son, seven at the time, led his best friend into a personal relationship with Christ. It was only a month later that his mother and father bent their knees and asked Jesus to be their Forgiver and Leader. I had the personal privilege of baptizing both of them. And it all began with my son, Derek, building a personal relationship with his best friend.

Through my experience with the Wrights I began to see a more natural and organic way to share the love of Christ. I found I was doing the mission of the church in the community where people far from

God lived and waited for someone to tell them about Jesus. I was doing more than when I was huddled with the already-convinced in the white-washed classrooms in the buildings known since my childhood as the church. These experiences were the seeds to CBSE.

What Is Community-Based Servant Evangelism?

CBSE is not the next new evangelism program! It is also more than doing random acts of kindness in Jesus' name, which some may call "Servant Evangelism." CBSE is intentional evangelism, which affects the lives of people who were headed toward a Christ-less eternity. It is systematic approaches to evangelism, which enable Christ-followers the possibilities of seeing their friends and neighbors begin relationships with Christ. CBSE is a philosophy of ministry and strategy of organizing the church that will influence ministry, events, and programs of the local church and, specifically, *the community.*

CBSE is going out to people who are far from God–where they live, play, work, and serve in our communities. Such an approach will mean a change of direction, or a change in invitation for your church. *The Relevant Church* authors challenge us when they write:

> We need to stop inviting people to Christian events as our only form of outreach. Instead, start inviting people to spend time where they already are. There is a choice to be made here. We can either try to bring a person into our setting–however uncomfortable they may feel–or we can spend time with an individual in their setting and sacrifice our comfort.[1]

Most churches in America are great places to bring people. However, many people who are far from God prefer to see a genuine difference demonstrated by our actions precisely because we are Christ-followers. Our purpose as co-mission with Christ is to see people come into a personal relationship with Him, not come inside our church buildings. Andy Stanley concluded, "Christ didn't commission us to become authorities so we could tell people how they ought to live. He called us to be influencers by the way we live, so people would want what we have."[2]

We want to describe the four key concepts in CBSE. We will explain each of these four words to give you an overall grasp of the scope and process of CBSE. We will then turn to the implementation of each concept in your church. Before we begin, however, we have a word of caution. Because of church leaders' tendency to establish "silos" for everything (placing items, ministries, programs into nice, neat compartments), you may be tempted to compartmentalize

CBSE as another silo in your arsenal of strategic weapons to win your community for Christ. For what we are talking about to have the most significant impact in your ministry, it cannot become another silo along with the worship/music ministry, small groups ministry, women's ministry, student's ministry, children's ministry, prayer ministry, etc. Unfortunately, churches continue to build new silos every year and never stop to develop pathways to intentionally interconnect them.

Here is what most church programs look like:

Many of Today's Churches

Youth   Children   Adult   Pre-School   Women   Men   Music   Sports

In this model, the church is a collection of silo ministries with staff hired to manage each silo. Turf wars, resource raids, volunteer gouging, and personal agendas become the discussion items for meetings that are more about conflict resolution among the managing parties than about stories of changed lives by Jesus. This structure creates many of the recurring problems in the lives of many churches today, and if one of the silos becomes larger than the others, conflict occurs at exponential rates. Just ask the youth pastor who wonders why the church organist makes more than he does and why he can't use the choir room as an overflow area for the growing number of students who have signed up for a weekend event at the church.

Community-Based Servant Evangelism Churches

Church

Here is a picture of a church that has adopted CBSE as its system for ministry. A single-silo church is the church of the twenty-first century. The single silo does not contain all the individual silos from the diagram above. This church exists as a single entity, built around a single focus. That focus, or purpose expressed in a single strategy, is the source for any and all ministries that the leaders create to carry that purpose throughout the church and into the community. Alan Hirsch has observed the reason we don't do church this way is because we have the wrong "software" running on the wrong "machines":

Many efforts to revitalize the church aim at simply adding or developing new programs or sharpening the theology and doctrinal base of the church. But seldom do we ever get to address the "hardware" or the "machine language" on which all this depends. This means that efforts to fundamentally reorient the church around its mission fail, because the foundational system, in this case the Christendom mode or understanding of the church, cancels out what the "software" is requiring.[3]

Churches can no longer allow ministries to create their own silos. Ministries must work together and find ways to support each other and track in a single direction. Programs, ministries, and events must cooperate in such a way that each enables the others to fulfill their purpose. We cannot consider any ministry successful if it negatively influences others. One test that will help you know if your church is a single-silo church or a multi-silo church is to answer this question, "How do you measure a ministry's effectiveness?" If you count attendance, number of volunteers, or the size of its budget, your church is most likely a multi-silo church.

We must quit fighting over resources inside the walls of our church buildings and get into the lives of those in the communities that surround us. Those communities, however, are moving targets. Our world is not the same as it was when we (most church leaders) grew up. My (Steve's) father was born, raised, and died in my hometown. My mother was born in Kentucky, but moved as a child to my hometown, where she lived the rest of her life. I was born and lived my first eighteen years in the same house, doing life with the same friends. Since matriculating at Southeast Missouri State University in 1971, I have lived in Kentucky, Maryland, Virginia, Mississippi, Arkansas, Colorado, and Texas. Today very few of us grow up and stay in the same community for our entire lives. Many Americans live in multiple places. If we are not moving, we are on the road or in the skies frequently. Jennifer Ashley, et al., surmise, "Because of the mobility and complexity of contemporary society, it's most appropriate to see 'church' as a multi-portal community—a web of all the relationships and activities, both local and global, in which I share kingdom vision, values, and practices with others."[4]

CBSE leads the Christ-follower into his or her community to be a salt and light servant in the name of Jesus. Our presence in the comings and goings of daily living are the platform from which we offer the life-changing message of Jesus. Who we are in the mission field matters to those who "hunger and thirst after righteousness." Jared Mackey reminds us:

> Each of us should be as concerned about who we are becoming, and what the community is becoming, because of our efforts. The nature of the ministry of Christ was a ministry of being. A ministry of presence. He changed lives, brought hope, and impacted lives for eternity in simply being fully in people's presence. Our actions, not the premeditated ones but rather the natural motions from our life, are the determining factor to what we truly believe. Our statements of desire to change the world do little unless they are accompanied by a consistent display of our beliefs.[5]

Jesus calls us to join Him in the mission field, not as saviors, but as sinners saved by grace who can lead their friends to Jesus and who humbly give a cup of water in His name.

Many churches celebrate a tremendous past. They have reached many people far from God and have developed them into devoted followers of Christ. They have planted successful churches and sent loved ones across oceans as missionaries. They have built hospitals and seminaries both in this country and around the world. They have met critical and urgent needs across planet Earth. However, churches and Christ-followers may have rested on the past so long that it has negatively influenced our ability to affect our current culture. If the church is to fulfill the Great Commandment and Great Commission in this season of His-story, we must, as Richard Philips writes, "…build on the things done right in the past. We build on the human relationships, the bonds of affection and trust and inspiration that lie waiting in our memories, in the people we have served and been served by, in the dreams that once filled us with purpose and resolution."[6]

Let's turn now to a description of CBSE by addressing each of its parts and how they integrate to provide a system of living the two Great C's.

Community

The first descriptive word in CBSE can have a dual meaning. One meaning comes from a buzzword heard around churches, which includes the word *community,* as in "biblical community." Speakers and writers refer to it as a key component of following Christ. Community in this sense is simply togetherness in Jesus' name, as described in Acts 2:42–47. According to Gilbert Bilezikian, or "Dr. B" to those closest to him, biblical community is a place where a person can know and be known, love and be loved, serve and be served, admonish and be admonished, and celebrate and be celebrated for who he or she is.[7] Dr. Bilezikian concludes, "Without community, there is no Christianity. Perfect community is to be found at the intersection of the two segments of the cross, where those who are reconciled with God can be reconciled together. Community is central to God's purposes for humankind."[8]

God exists in community. In the opening pages of *Leading the Team Based Church,* George Cladis reminds us of the ancient picture of the Trinity's "circle dance" and the perfect image of community it portrays.[9] God placed in people a desire to be in community with others. Therefore, it should not be a surprise that people desire community and authentic relationships. Through research, we know that a baby deprived of love can physically die. In his book *Evangelism Out of the Box,* Rick Richardson challenges us, "People are looking first for community to belong to rather than message to believe in. They are looking for a safe place to work out their sense of identity and self."[10] It follows, then, that leading those far from God to Jesus is best done through authentic relationships in genuine community.

However, "community" in CBSE is more than a sense of togetherness. It is where we do life, where we live. In *An Emergent Manifesto of Hope,* Ryan Bolger shares the following: "A kingdomlike church follows God's mission into the world because that is where God's mission is located. Such a church does not create a 'come-to-us' structure and convince others to become members—God's reign is much bigger than the membership rolls of local churches."[11] It is where we work, where we connect with people in malls and stores, ball fields, schools, and on sidewalks. Community in this context is a group of people living in the same locality with common interests. While diversity and multiculturalism are on the rise even in America's suburbs, the people who live in a particular locale most likely share the values of their township, if not shared experiences through involvement in daily life.

Community, in an Acts 1:8 paradigm for missions, is our Jerusalem. It is where God desires us to become individually involved to live out His Great Commandment and Great Commission. Jesus insisted His apprentices were to be salt and light in their communities first. It is here that Jesus told us not to hide our light under a basket (Mt. 5:15). The ins and outs of daily life in our locale are where we interact with our neighbors and the place we earn the privilege of hearing, "Well done, good and faithful [servant]. You were faithful with a few things, I will put you in charge of many things; enter into the joy of your master" (Mt. 25:23).

The "community" aspect of CBSE is, at its core, about making a difference in the name of Jesus when you do life by serving those who share a similar culture and daily experiences. In *The Relevant Church,* the authors state:

> To make an impact in the twenty-something culture, leaders need to be involved in "real" culture, not just Christian "sub-culture" events. If you are a musician, then you should be in the music clubs performing on weekends, not just in Christian coffeehouses. If you are a comedian, you should be working in the comedy clubs during the week as a way of meeting people and impacting the community. If you are an athlete, join a league and play with a random group of people, not just a church league. We encourage people to use their gifts not just "in here," but "out there."[12]

It is "out there," in the darkness and among real people, that Christ-followers are the light of the world. It is in the community where Christ-followers have the opportunity to "spice" up conversations as the Savior's salt. Out there is where we can change the flavor and taste of the lifestyles of the poor and unknown. Andy Stanley wrote, "The truth is our secular pursuits have more kingdom potential than our religious ones. For it is in the realm of our secular pursuits that secular people are watching."[13] Alan Hirsch adds, "Discipleship is determined by the relation to Christ himself not by mere conformity to impersonal commands. The context of this is not in the classroom (where 'teaching' normally takes place), or even in the church, but in the world."[14]

Living as salt and light servants is how we connect and build authentic relationships with people who are far from God. Many Christ-followers do not even know someone who is outside a relationship with God. I (Gene) recall a conversation with a church member who finally confessed, "I don't have any friends who aren't Christians. All my friends go to church."

When I heard this church member's confession, I knew why he didn't grasp my messages on seeing people as Jesus sees them. He had come to me to complain that my messages were no longer "touching" him as they had when he first came to the church. He wondered why my interests seemed to have turned from helping him grow to talking about the people who weren't yet at the church. I tried to explain that a sign of Christian maturity was a love for the lost–it wasn't about knowing the latest "endtimes" theory or "embedded Bible code."[15]

Church members who live and breathe in a Christian subculture soon forget the important reality of befriending those far from God. They are more comfortable with their "own kind" than with those who are different than they are. However, speaking the Word in relationship is how God changes people's hearts.

The authors of *Primal Leadership* state:

> The art of handling relationships well, then, begins with authenticity: acting from one's genuine feelings. Once leaders have attuned to their own vision and values, steadied in the positive emotional range, and tuned into the emotions of the group, then relationship management skills let them interact in ways that catalyze resonance. Rather, *relationship management is friendliness with a purpose:* moving people in the right direction, whether that's agreement on a marketing strategy or enthusiasm about a new project.[16] (Italics added)

Christ-followers must influence their culture not simply by making stands against governmental decisions or by protesting local referendums, but by building genuine relationships, one life at a time. When we think of church as a series of relational connections rather than a single congregation meeting, then we can best impact the culture of those far from God with the Good News of Jesus.

Some pastors and key church leaders have raised at least two areas of concern related to intentionally placing members in the community. They are usually phrased as questions. The first is, "What happens if and when a church member or members begin serving in community and civic organizations and they 'blow it'? Won't that create a greater problem?"

Our answer usually goes something like this. "We can understand your concern. But, just because the church encourages their members to serve in the community does not mean they will be even more inclined to blow it than Christians do now. Church members blow it each and everyday. Just because we encourage their involvement does not mean they will blow it more often than they already do." The problem is not Christ-followers who "blow it," but rather *our* failure to help people stay out of, or deal with, the situations in which they did not honor God with their actions, words, and intentions.

The second question pastors often raise is, "What if they choose to serve in community or civic organizations we are not in agreement with?" This can possibly happen as you release members into their communities to follow their gifts and passions. However, by relying on the Holy Spirit and your church's small groups, their service can be leveraged as a teachable moment. Many churches rely more on policies, procedures, and their church constitution and bylaws than they do on the Holy Spirit.

We do have a word of caution for churches who are considering deploying people into their communities. It is not easy. People have a tendency to drift back toward old ways of thinking. Ken Blanchard and Phil Hodges said it this way: "If pressure [to be involved in the community] is taken off, people will revert to old behaviors."[17] Jared Mackey, ministry pastor at the Next Level Church in Englewood, Colorado, said in a personal conversation, "There is an incredible battle to keep people out there because we tend to drift toward a fortress mentality." A fortress mentality is exactly why we find the church in America in its current state. To deploy members in the community therefore will be a constant battle, even after the philosophy of ministry has taken hold. Joseph Myers may sum up the idea of community best when he states, "Churches don't become legendary on the community grapevine via reporting of numbers. They become legendary through the sharing of their story of mission within the community."[18]

Legacy Church, where Gene is the senior pastor, is known on the community grapevine for the Helping Hands ministry and English Language Program. Legacy Church is known as one of several key churches that the city of Plano recognized as supporters of the city's efforts to care for the survivors of Hurricanes Katrina and Rita. For Gene and Legacy Church, their reputation with the community is more important than their reputation in the Christian subculture of Dallas and Fort Worth.

Based

CBSE is a matter of focus. Something "based" indicates the intentionality of where it is placed. For example, countries strategically locate a military base to enable their soldiers to engage the enemy more easily. A "base" is where armies supply and train their soldiers. Author Frank Viola stated, "God did not form the church to be an end in itself. The church is a means for the fulfillment of something far greater."[19] Bases represent the countries that placed them there. Their relationship with the locals can be either hostile or reciprocal. For example, the U.S. presence in Iraq was well received in some parts of the country, while in other places U.S. troops constantly came under fire by insurgents. Presence does not always mean acceptance, and, like military troops stationed on foreign soil, so the church must not only deploy its people into the local culture, but they must work diligently to maintain a positive reputation with those where they are based.

I (Gene) have articulated a vision for churches to become "mission outposts." Such a church has "a mission field focus and equips and sends its members as missionaries into the world around them."[20] These mission outposts are similar to the one Barnabas and Saul served in Antioch. Acts 11:19–30 and 13:1–3 provide the model for the mission outposts that organically sprang up throughout the known world through the travels of Paul the Apostle and the work of the communities of faith wherever he went or wrote.

Christ demonstrated a "community-based" ministry while on earth. John, "the disciple whom Jesus loved," revealed to us that Jesus was "in the world, and the world was made through Him, and the world did not know Him" (Jn. 1:10). Jesus called his followers to go to their towns and kinsmen to tell and live out the Good News of His coming. It follows that to be Great Commandment and Great Commission people we are to be "in the world" and to base our church's ministries there.

Additionally, the concept of "based" can refer to the culture of the church. Whether the church understands this or not, a church operates in two cultures: a culture for those who compose the church and a different culture for those in the community surrounding where the church gathers. The more the two cultures are alike, the greater likelihood that they can fulfill the Great Commandment and the Great Commission. This statement is so very important that it requires repeating. *The more a church's culture reflects the culture of its community, the greater the likelihood it will fulfill the Great Commandment and Great Commission in that culture.*

It is important that you understand our hearts clearly on this. We are *not* saying the local church needs to become secular or that it should condone acts or practices that are counter- or anti-Christian. We do *not* believe that churches should take on the *sinful nature* of the community around them. We *do* believe that the local church must wrestle with and address the same issues and values of its cultural base. The church members in any locale must *not* offer "other world" responses to real problems and felt needs in their community to the point that they speak a different language than the "natives." When Jesus' called-out ones reflect the real-life struggles and problems of those with whom they live and demonstrate the freedom, joy, and hope Jesus has brought them, then they can impact the culture in which they have been planted. What would it be like if the church was able to affect such a cultural change that sociologists would come and study why the community is so loving, caring, and compassionate? What would it say about the power of the Gospel if when the sociologists came, they discovered Jesus?

A great deal of Steve's time and energy is spent with church planters. He has found their dreams and vision are difficult to contain as they build their core group, get funding, and launch their churches. But, as the years pass, the original vision and passion sometimes lose momentum. Too often the work of these planters sputters and dies before they realize what God wrote on their hearts to do. The churches that can keep the vision and dream burning white-hot are the ones we read about, and then travel to in order to attend their conferences. What is the difference? Sometimes it is what Louis Gerstner observed: "Successful institutions almost always develop strong cultures that reinforce those elements that make the institution great. They reflect the environment from which they emerged."[21]

As you implement CBSE, it allows you a new beachhead from which to launch Christlike influence in your community. Possibly the greatest military invasion in world history was D-Day in World War II. The Allies sailed across the English Channel to establish a beachhead or base on the European continent. From the established beachheads they would launch missions that would result in the Allies entering Germany and ending World War II. Without establishing the beachhead, which meant putting men on the ground and in harm's way, the end of the war could have turned out much differently. Similarly, as we deploy church members into the community as salt and light, we have the opportunity to establish a "beachhead," or base, from which we launch the Great Commission.

To continue our D-Day analogy, General Eisenhower knew an air assault alone would not establish the beachhead or base. Air bombardments and shells launched from ally ships off the coast were critically important to the success of the assault, but it took men who were willing to sacrifice their lives on the beaches to establish the base so the mission could be fulfilled. Enemy bullets fly in the danger zone, or, in the language of the Bible, "the flaming arrows of the evil one" (Eph. 6:16). Friends and loved ones face grave dangers as they establish beachheads against the enemy. Around the world today, many become martyrs in their fight against Satan and satanic forces. But what other alternative do we really have? We could determine that the cost would be so high that we turn our churches into monasteries. This cloistering of saints has been a strategy of the church before. Or, we could decide to climb down off the large transport ship into an amphibious landing boat and circle aimlessly in the English Channel, never arriving on the beach and facing the danger of actually engaging the enemy. Too many churches in the U.S. seem to prefer this strategy. Or, we could once and for all determine the *only* way to fulfill our mission is to get out of the boat and onto the beach to fight the enemy and free the indigenous peoples from its tyranny. Our cry is, "Join us in the assault ship as we establish the beachhead base to launch small parties and individuals into our communities to free the locals and establish Christ's presence among them."

Servant

Jesus made it clear from the beginning of his public ministry that He would not fit the mold of Messiah for which many of the Jews hoped. He allowed children to interrupt Him. He came into close contact with and healed people who had leprosy—basically the HIV/AIDS victims of the day. He went home with Jewish tax collectors, unbecoming behavior for a religious man. He spent time with and honored women. He looked for ways to serve people. His first recorded miracle was to help out a wedding host by turning water into wine (Jn. 2).

A question that few church leaders have the intestinal fortitude to ask is, How can the church regain a strategic place in our communities? Or, have we so culturally turned inward we are incapable of ever looking outside our walls? "For the church to really serve as a 'city on a hill' to those outside," observe Pagitt and Jones, "it must dynamically interact with the surrounding culture in ways that make sense to those outside."[22]

Prior to the more in-depth discussion on the "servant," or "service," aspect of CBSE, it is important for us to understand the propensity Americans have to serve. "In the year 2000, according to the leadership forum Independent Sector, roughly 84 million adults aged 21 and older volunteered 15.5 billion hours"[23] (roughly 184 hours per person for the year). The basic issue for churches and Christ-followers is, *Where* are our people serving? Are they serving our organizations and programs, or are they serving community and civic organizations? Granted, many are serving both. However, the important question remains: As they serve in community and civic organizations, are they serving from the "salt and light" prospective?

Jesus surely upset many of his followers' expectations when he washed their feet (Jn. 13). The symbol of God in Jesus' movement was a towel and washbasin, not a scepter or crown. Aubrey Malphurs writes, "We'll serve others humbly only to the degree that we love them. And the dirt on their feet will test our love for them. If we don't love them, we'll take up the leadership towel only to toss in that towel quickly when it gets a little dirty."[24] The quintessential picture of Jesus as a servant leader emerged when He washed His disciple's feet. Could it possibly be that Christ-followers are the most like Jesus when they serve people? Erwin McManus agrees: "When we move ourselves to the place of servanthood, we join God in His eternal purpose. When we serve others, we look strangely like God."[25]

Jesus' demonstrations of compassion for people fill the pages of the gospel stories. God's Son intentionally sought ways to serve people. Rusaw and Swanson ask, "Imagine Jesus going out into towns and villages during His public ministry and proclaiming His gospel without accompanying acts of healing and helping (Mt. 9:35). Do we really think our savior would have gained a hearing (much less following) or established the credibility of His message—without displaying some proof that this gospel was real?"[26] Our communities wonder the same thing about our churches. When we claim to be followers of Jesus, they want to know where are the "accompanying acts of healing and helping"?

As we have already noted, our relationship with Christ is the motivation for an authentic love for people that propels us to help them experience Jesus' promise, "I came that [you] may have life, and have it abundantly" (Jn. 10:10b). People outside a relationship with Christ should make our hearts beat out of our chests because we want them to experience what a personal relationship with Christ can mean. McManus observes, "Love produces servanthood. Servanthood sees sacrifice as a privilege. When we are known by love, we are known for the towel wrapped around our waist."[27]

One of the many side benefits of service to the community in the name of Jesus is that it allows Christ-followers to affect people they might not ever have an opportunity to influence otherwise. We know, "Servants get invited places into which the mighty can't force their way."[28] Salt and Light Servants do not wear disguises to sneak behind enemy lines. Servants who have apprenticed themselves to the Servant Jesus enter their community to serve like their Master because that is who they are, not because that is what they do on Saturday mornings instead of reading a newspaper at their favorite coffee shop.

Historically the New Testament Church looked for ways to serve those in the community. Christ-followers eagerly assisted people who were in need. One of the first conflicts in the church arose from their efforts to feed widows of a certain ethnic group (Acts 6). Now in America, rather than people turning to the church for help with their basic needs, state and national governmental agencies assist more people who are in desperate need. While some vagabonds have discovered the network of churches who give handouts in their towns, most people in need turn to the government first for help. Clothes closets and food pantries in churches have in many cases become nothing more than a token of our compassion and service to the community.

However, the tide is changing. Over the past twenty years, churches and parachurch agencies have begun to pick up some of the responsibility to meet the personal needs of those living in their communities. Churches such as First Baptist Church of Leesburg, Florida, have established a wide-ranging frontline ministry to those in need. The twenty-five-year ministry of Charles Roesel has led the church to serve people in need with a purpose: to introduce people to Jesus Christ. He refers to their ministry to the homeless, the hungry, unwed mothers, and abused women and children as "ministry evangelism."

> Ministry evangelism is simply caring for persons in the name of Jesus Christ. It is meeting persons at the point of their need and ministering to them physically and spiritually. The intent of ministry evangelism is to present the good news of God's love in order to introduce the person to Jesus.[29]

First Baptist Church of Leesburg has committed large sums of money and volunteers to run these ministries. They have assisted thousands of people in need and led many into a personal relationship with Christ. As a result, they also have touched and motivated many churches across the country to explore the possibility of beginning ministry-based evangelism in their churches. Ministry evangelism in Leesburg is an example of servant evangelism as we envision it.

Would you like to investigate the needs in your community but don't know where to start? Check the Web site http://www.factfinder. census.gov and The United Way Web site (http://www.unitedway. org; click on: *volunteer connection*).

The Dallas Morning News, on a regular basis, lists volunteer opportunities for the metroplex. In the November 28, 2007, edition, twenty different opportunities for individuals to volunteer were listed. The list includes: crime prevention, receptionists for refugees, marketing assistants, client intake volunteers, ESL volunteer training, help seniors with finances and assessment coordinators, etc. Each of these opportunities provides countless opportunities for Christ-followers to build relationships with people far from God in the community. Each of these provides church members an opportunity to make a positive impact in their community meeting real needs. Each of these represents a fantastic opportunity to be salt and light. Why do more churches not see these opportunities to volunteer in their communities as God-initiated opportunities to increase the numerical size of heaven?

The "service," or "servant," aspect of CBSE can take the form of additional yet just as important roles as meeting the physical needs of others. Christ-followers can also engage people far from God in their communities who have pressing tangible felt needs, such as food, clothing, housing, and care. You may address less pressing but just as real felt needs, such as when you find that your community:

- has a need for a passionate man or woman to coach a Little League team
- needs people to work with racetrack management to provide services for race fans who camp out for the weekend races
- searches for a friendly face to greet people as they enter a hospital to check on a loved one or close friend
- must have someone to interpret for immigrants as they leave the U.S. Customs Office
- needs a person to assist foreigners as they seek homes in America
- needs help renovating or building homes in your city
- has single mothers who need car repairs and cannot afford them.

Contact your local city manager's office to find the specific ways in which you can help. These needs are not on the same level as food, clothing, medical assistance, or lodging; however, all of these offer Christ-followers a *connection point*, which can be developed into an opportunity to demonstrate the love of Jesus in tangible ways. To serve as salt and light servants with towels over our arms to meet needs can be the initial step for many on a spiritual journey that ends with them asking Christ to be their Leader and Forgiver.

John Miller, worship pastor at the Next Level Church, said, "We don't often consider serving those around us as an act of worship, but consider that the basic intent of worship is to bring honor, reverence, and admiration to God. We can worship God by taking care of His children."[30] We believe worship is a lifestyle, and serving others is surely an act of worship.

Evangelism

Modern evangelicals molded evangelism into a wide variety of methods and strategies that primarily sought to get the "data" of the gospel shared with those who did not know it. The results have been everything from presenting memorized outlines or manipulating a picture cube to present the Gospel to strangers to organizing neighborhood block parties for the purpose of building relationship to tell the facts of the gospel. We concur with Rusaw and Swanson when they surmise, "In our evangelistic zeal, we often think people just need more or better information in order to believe. But, we fail to realize that what they really long for is authenticity. Fewer are asking, 'What must I do to be saved?' Instead their question is, 'What can I do to make my life work?'"[31] The pragmatism of postmoderns has replaced the categories of the Enlightenment. Evangelism includes facts, but they seem now to follow practical service, not preclude it.

Churches have attempted many varied approaches to get the Word out to others. Direct mail, confrontational evangelism, seeker services, seeker small groups, and event evangelism all seek to increase the numerical size of heaven. In addition, churches embrace new and improved evangelism-training tools perfected by a church in a culture different from their own. They hope that it may be the missing ingredient that will be the catalyst for numerical growth. In the process, we have lost how Jesus showed people why He came. Sarah Cunningham sums up our feelings:

> This rehearsed style of evangelism often seems to run contrary to what actually draws people to God. Most people in my life are only marginally influenced by my memorized salvation verbiage. Quite the opposite, I win or loose most debates about the reality of God based on whether or not God is reflected in my reality. My best evangelism is prolonged life-on-life contact.[32]

Evangelism is simply to "tell good news." Car salesmen and infomercial personalities are evangelists for their products. We become evangelists for the latest great film we saw over the weekend when, on Monday morning, we tell others, "You've got to see this movie."

Jesus was an evangelist because he not only told people "the kingdom of heaven" was "at hand," but also because he demonstrated what that looked like in their daily existence. Jesus modeled an evangelistic lifestyle we want to emulate. He often met a physical, emotional, or spiritual need and then told those watching why it happened and who was responsible. Other times, he answered a question or request and entered into dialogue with those present.

Yes, sometimes we must speak first, but many times we must act first. As Christ-followers, evangelism is not an obligation we must do to keep our place in the family. It is an opportunity to deepen our personal relationship with Christ and partner with Him to capture the hearts of men, women, boys, and girls. Ron Lewis used to say, "All lasting church growth begins with the command of God followed by the needs of those who need to be reached."[33]

We know the vast majority of Christ-followers desire to be used by God to bring others into relationship with Him. The problem is not desire! Too often our churches have developed such an extensive reliance on event and church programs that most Christ-followers do not have an opportunity to spend quality time with people far from God. Growing inside the church buildings and seeking our own felt needs with those who think, talk, and dress like us excludes us from the key conversations necessary to address the deep longings of those in our network of relationships. The sociologist Ray Oldenburg has noted:

> Cut off from the primary groups that nurtured their forbearers and gave them a sense of identity, large numbers of Americans are looking for someone to tell them who they are or who they should be. Depending on their means and level of sophistication, they may enroll in courses that promise to develop "personality" or enter some form of therapy. But most are seeking an acceptable label or the secret to gaining power over others, rather than seeking to know themselves.[34]

Let us ask you a few questions: "With how many people far from God do you regularly spend time?" "Are you so tied up with church stuff that you do not have any time available to spend with anyone but Christ-followers?" "Are you indeed living life hoping that those far from Him will reach out to us first so we can give the 'speech' we learned at the last evangelism training course?"

Not only must we get near to and build relationships with people far from God, we must also understand their values, or lack of values.

Bill Easum observed, "Most pre-Christians have two distinguishing characteristics. They have grown up outside any influence of Christianity, and they have been mentored more by their peers than by their parents. As a result, they are intensely tolerant of a vast variety of viewpoints and gods."[35] As Christ-followers, we should not allow our familiarity with the things of God to be the only platforms from which we show Christ's love.

As was customary at that time, Jesus' father, Joseph, taught Him carpentry skills. Jesus learned the skills of molding freshly cut timber into usable implements, such as plows and yokes. Although Jesus had years of knowledge and experience as a carpenter, how many wood and carpentry parables do the gospels contain? Did Jesus use carpentry illustrations when He taught the "Sermon on the Mount?" The easiest approach Jesus could have taken was to use the things He was most familiar with. Instead, Jesus leveraged agricultural information because His culture was knowledgeable on the topic. If Jesus would have used carpentry as an illustration, the people may or may not have understood. He sought the most common denominator among the majority of His listeners to build a bridge to the Good News of His coming.

Jesus also understood that what catches the eye of a person far from God is not necessarily words, but a demonstration of Truth in the lives of those He touched. Easum continues, "The primary struggle of the pre-Christian age is to come to an understanding of what it is about our relationship with Jesus that the world cannot live without."[36] Are church members living in such a way that they demonstrate something people far from God cannot live without?

The Evangelistic Journey

Several years ago, my mentor, Ron Lewis, and I (Steve) took an instrument previously developed by Charles Engle and developed it further. We attempted to make it more relevant to our current culture. Take a minute and study Table 2.1 on the next page. It is the scale of the evangelistic journey for most people.

The Evangelistic Journey visually demonstrates several important issues regarding CBSE and the local church. First, for an increasing number of people in our communities that are −10, −9, −8,…simply opening our doors each Sunday will not work. Many church leaders are aware of this, but it has not resulted in a change in methodology. Second, evangelism is a process, not an event. It takes time to address concerns and questions for a −10 or −9 individual to consider "spiritual things."

TABLE 2.1

The Evangelistic Journey

-10 Atheist–Agnostic
- 9 Initial questions regarding a creator
- 8 Believes a creator exists
- 7 Explores the Bible and other related data
- 6 Has basic Bible knowledge
- 5 Interested in what the Bible says
- 4 Knows and understands some of the basics
- 3 Senses the personal implications of the gospel and is receptive to application of the gospel to his/her life
- 2 Desires to act on the gospel
- 1 Asks Christ to be the Forgiver and Leader of his/her life

Crossing the Line of Faith

+1 Ponders what has happened
+2 Feels excited about new life
+3 Assimilates into small group and church
+4 Faces spiritual failures in self and others
+5 Senses personal need for the will of God
+6 Life is enriched by prayer and Bible study
+7 Discovers spiritual gifts and has desire to use them for the Kingdom vision
+8 Accepts leadership or servant role in the church
+9 Involved in stewardship plan of the church
+10 Fully devoted follower (salt and light servant)

Third, out in the community is the only place we will connect with –10, –9, –8 people of our communities. The –10, –9, and –8 are not likely to show up at your church. Fourth, it is important for Christ-followers, especially small group leaders, to understand where their friends or acquaintances are in their personal spiritual journeys. Finally, the Evangelistic Journey is a visual of both the Great Commandment and Great Commission.

Nurturing people along this journey will not be an easy road. Leaders by nature create conflict as they challenge the status quo and invite people to trust them enough to go to a place they would not go on their own. Ronald Heifetz and Marty Linsky warn leaders, "If you are to be authentic and effective, you must play your role in accordance with what you believe so that your passions infuse your work. You need to realize that you cannot have it both ways. If you are attacked, discredited, ostracized, or fired, you may feel that you have experienced a kind of assassination. But you cannot expect people to seriously consider your idea without accepting the possibility that they will challenge it."[39] Jesus encountered conflict as He introduced the presence of the kingdom of heaven into a religiously saturated culture, but He persisted to complete the journey of salvation for all who would trust Him. We should do the same.

CBSE involves a Christ-follower who serves others out of his or her passion (what you would really like to do), using one's spiritual gifts at connection points of need in the community to demonstrate the love of Jesus to others as a salt and light servant. This way of being the called-out ones by Jesus will release a large percentage of volunteers to be salt and light in the community. It is trusting that the Holy Spirit impassions a Christ-follower's heart to love those in their matrix of friendships as they are salt and light.

Administratively, CBSE reduces the church's events and ongoing programs to allow people to be deployed into their daily lives to exercise their passions and gifts. People will serve out of their passion, regardless of where that is. Joseph Myers tells us, "People...want to know that you have chosen them first and foremost because of who they are, not to fulfill a strategic master plan.[40] CBSE elevates members as ministers, ordained by God and empowered by His Spirit, to be priests to their friends. Priests are simply those who represent the needs of the people to God and God to the people. Pastors and church staff discover their roles are not managers of a department but equippers of co-workers to do the work of the ministry. To do things as we always have done them will produce the same results.

CBSE is effective individually or collectively, as small group members are deployed to serve shoulder to shoulder in their communities. This way of living (church) allows small groups to serve a community agency or program, a governmental agency, or even a business. Members become ministers and missionaries, and their neighborhoods become the mission field in which God invites them to demonstrate His presence and love.

What Does a Developed Salt and Light Servant Look Like?

CBSE is also a vehicle to mature people into devoted followers of Christ. The maturation process is more than having members involved in more Bible studies. It is more than attending special doctrinal studies. It is more than disseminating more information. Developing devoted followers of Christ is about spiritual transformation. We believe the best and most effective strategy to transform Christ-follower's lives is to involve them in purposeful service. We know that most maturing Christ-followers know far more about the Bible than they have incorporated into their lives. Application of what they know will not only grow them in the likeness of Jesus; it will also be a visible witness to Christ to their friends and those in need.

What does a maturing salt and light servant look like? We believe local churches need to take a break from managing their programs to define the characteristics of a devoted follower of Christ. What does a church want its members to become? What does a fully devoted follower of Christ look like? What is our strategy as a church for developing people?

Several churches across America have developed lists of characteristics toward which they intentionally develop people. Willow Creek Community Church has defined a devoted follower as someone who demonstrates the five "G's": Grace, Growth, Groups, Gift, and Good stewardship. The leadership of Vista Ridge Baptist Church in Carrollton, Texas, set aside forty-five days to read the New Testament and catalogue the characteristics of a devoted follower of Christ. The characteristics they listed were:

> Faith, humble, Servant, Boldness, Grace, Reliance upon the Holy Spirit, an understanding of Heaven/Hell, fasting, love God and love others, unity, involvement in the body, demonstrates spiritual wisdom, a listener, demonstrates forgiveness toward others, joyful, gives of their time and financial resources in keeping to Acts 2, solitude, accepting, lives in biblical community, shares their faith regularly.

The strength of this approach is the involvement of many individuals in developing such a list. To copy a list that another church has developed can short-circuit the maximum benefit of such a list created for your church. We suggest you take time to create your own end picture of what you want your people to become.

When he was pastor of Pantego Bible Church, Randy Frazee defined a devoted follower by identifying thirty Core Competencies. (See chart on next page.)

Finally, CBSE is a philosophy of ministry, not the newest approach or church program to implement. The ministry philosophy must flow through every ministry, worship experience, discipleship process, and leadership meeting. The strength of CBSE is that its philosophy becomes part of the DNA of a church without changing any program or curriculum the church is currently using. Through the remainder of this leadership manual, we will refer to *Network* and *Just Walk Across the Room* as possible tools to be used to assist with the implementation of CBSE. However, because this is philosophy-driven and not program-driven, those curriculum pieces are not necessary for a church to deploy a CBSE model.

BELIEFS	PRACTICES	VIRTUES
Trinity	Worship	Love
Salvation	Prayer	Joy
Authority of Bible	Bible Study	Peace
Personal God	Single-mindedness	Patience
Identity in Christ	Biblical Community	Kindness
Church	Spiritual Gifts	Faithfulness
Humanity	Giving away my time	Gentleness
Compassion	Giving away my money	Self-control
Eternity	Giving away my faith	Hope
Stewardship	Giving away my life	Humility[41]

Therefore, if the local church previously has selected a spiritual gift inventory other than the spiritual gift inventory in Gene Wilkes' *Jesus on Leadership,* the implementation of CBSE requires a church to make minimal changes. If a local church currently is using any credible tool as its evangelism-training curriculum, the CBSE philosophy could be the piece of the puzzle missing in seeing large numbers of people becoming Christ-followers.

QUESTIONS FOR CONSIDERATION AND DISCUSSION

1. Is your church a single- or multi-silo church? What steps can we take to begin moving the culture of our church into a single silo?
2. List the intentional actions currently taken by your church to engage your surrounding community?
3. Has your church established a "base" in your community? If your church were not based in your community, would the community miss you? Why or why not?

4. Is your community "more abundant" because of your service in the community? Is your church known in the community as a group of people with towels over their arms ready to serve?

5. Are your members currently leveraging their service in community and civic organizations for Kingdom growth?

Notes

[1]Jennifer Ashley, Mike Bickle, Mark Driscoll, and Mike Howerton, *The Relevant Church* (Lake Mary, Fla.: Relevant Media Group, 2004), 103–4.

[2]Andy Stanley, *Visioneering* (Sisters, Oreg.: Multnomah, 1999), 190.

[3]Alan Hirsch, *The Forgotten Ways* (Grand Rapids: Brazos Press, 2006), 54.

[4]Ashley, Bickle, Driscoll, and Howerton, *The Relevant Church,* 144.

[5]Jared Mackey, "The Road of Ministry" in *Eternity,* The Next Level Church newsletter, November 2000.

[6]Richard D. Phillips, *The Heart of an Executive: Lessons on Leadership from the Life of David* (New York: Galilee Books, 1999), 243.

[7]Gilbert Bilezikian, *Community 101* (Grand Rapids: Zondervan, 1997).

[8]Ibid., 35.

[9]George Cladis, *Leading the Team Based Church* (San Francisco: Jossey-Bass, 1999), 3.

[10]Rick Richardson, *Evangelism Out of the Box* (Downers Grove, Ill.: InterVarsity Press, 2000), 48.

[11]Doug Pagitt and Tony Jones, *An Emergent Manifesto of Hope* (Grand Rapids: Baker Books, 2007), 134.

[12]Ashley, Bickle, Driscoll and Howerton, *The Relevant Church,* 103.

[13]Stanley, *Visioneering,* 225.

[14]Hirsch, *The Forgotten Ways,* 113.

[15]C. Gene Wilkes, *Paul on Leadership* (Nashville: LifeWay, 2004), 50.

[16]Daniel Goleman, Richard Boyatzis, and Annie McKee, *Primal Leadership* (Boston: Harvard Business School Press, 2002), 51.

[17]Ken Blanchard and Phil Hodges, *The Servant Leader* (Nashville: J. Countryman, 2003), 67.

[18]Joseph Myers, *Organic Community* (Grand Rapids: Baker Books, 2007), 80.

[19]Frank Viola, *Rethinking the Wineskin* (Gainesville: Present Testimony Ministry, 2001), 109.

[20]Wilkes, *Paul on Leadership,* 58.

[21]Louis V. Gerstner Jr., *Who Says Elephants Can't Dance?* (New York: Harper Collins Publishers, 2002), 182.

[22]Pagitt and Jones, *An Emergent Manifesto,* 133.

[23]Albert L. Winseman, *Growing an Engaged Church* (New York: Gallup Press, 2007), 74.

[24]Aubrey Malphurs, *Being Leaders* (Grand Rapids: Baker Books, 2003), 42.

[25]Erwin Raphael McManus, *Uprising: A Revolution of the Soul* (Nashville: Thomas Nelson Publishers, 2003), 251.

[26]Rick Rusaw and Eric Swanson, *The Externally Focused Church* (Loveland: Group Publishing, 2004), 7.

[27]Erwin Raphael McManus, *An Unstoppable Force* (Loveland: Group Publishing, 2001), 159.

[28]Rusaw and Swanson, *Externally Focused Church,* 62.

[29]Donald A. Atkinson and Charles L. Roesel, *Meeting Needs Sharing Christ* (Nashville: LifeWay , 1995), 10.

[30]John Miller, *Eternity: Ministry and Worship,* The Next Level Church Newsletter, November 2000.

[31]Rusaw and Swanson, *Externally Focused Church,* 28.

[32]Sarah Cunningham, *Dear Church* (Grand Rapids: Zondervan, 2006), 86.

[33]Ron S. Lewis, used by permission.

[34]Ray Oldenburg, *The Great Good Place: Cafes, Coffee Shops, Bookstores, Bars, Hair Salons and Other Hangouts at the Heart of a Community* (New York: Marlowe and Company, 1999), 292.

[35]Bill Easum, *Leadership on the Other Side* (Nashville: Abingdon Press, 2000), 72.

[36]Ibid., 77.

[37]Ronald A. Heifetz and Marty Linsky, *Leadership on the Line* (Boston: Harvard Business School, 2002), 190.

[38]Myers, *Organic Community,* 62.

[39]Heifetz and Linsky, *Leadership on the Line.*

[40]Myers, *Organic Community.*

[41]Randy Frazee, *The Christian Life Profile: A Discipleship Tool to Access Christian Beliefs* (Arlington: Creative Leadership Ministries, 1998), 11.

5

It Takes Salt and Light Servants

Communities in Schools (CIS) works with at-risk students with the goal of keeping them in school. The Village Church, Highland Village, Texas, recently opened up a second campus in Denton, Texas, and discovered the graduation rate of incoming freshmen at Denton High School was only 59.7 percent. The pastor and leaders of The Village Church encouraged members and regular attendees to volunteer to become mentors for the at-risk students through CIS (http://silentepidemic.org). More than 100 mentors now meet weekly with at-risk students at Denton High School, providing love, encouragement, motivation, and an opportunity to be "salt and light" to teachers, students, and parents.

The Great Commandment is our motivation as the people of God to love one another. The Great Commission is our mandate to take that love to all peoples–*ethnics*, if you transliterate the original Greek word. Jesus told the eleven awestruck disciples on the side of the hill that as they went about the rest of their lives, they were to "make disciples of all people groups, baptizing them...and teaching them" (Mt. 28:19, paraphrase). How can this command best be accomplished? Christ-followers have tried a variety of methods for nearly two thousand years, which have resulted in many successes and many failures. In the past twenty years, the focus has been on the educational side of the equation. "Experiencing God," "The Mind of Christ," Navigators "2.7 Series," Beth Moore's Bible study materials, and "Master Life" are all examples of an educational method for making disciples. The assumption has been, if we give people the "Truth" and if we package God's Word around essential biblical doctrines, values, and principles, then this accumulated information will result in someone known as a "disciple." For some this method is effective. However, for the vast majority of Christ-followers, information alone does not result in spiritual transformation.

I (Gene) have found that when a church chooses an information-based methodology to "make disciples," issues of personal preference and alignment of "curriculum" surface. Even when a carefully prepared outline of materials that follow a disciple-making path exists, you will hear from those in the groups, "We don't like that topic," or, "We did that last year. Is there anything else we can study?" or, "We just did a study on marriage. Do we have to do one on family, too?" Or, my favorite is, "We just want to study a book of the Bible," which usually leaves the teacher to pick his or her favorite book of the Bible to teach. Having no plan to develop disciples often results in a hodgepodge of topics that usually circulate around who read the latest Christian bestseller. The question for those leading the disciple-making process then becomes, "How do we equip our leaders? Are they teachers or coaches?"

We have begun to observe church leaders drift away from an educationally focused method to an experiential method for developing disciples of Jesus. This methodology incorporates educational materials, but it also includes service in the community as the context to live out the expression of a life in relationship to Christ. Will this varied focus result in a larger percentage of Christians becoming devoted followers of Christ? The verdict is still out. This varied approach we believe will result in a larger percentage of Christians becoming devoted followers of Christ.

The gospels indicate clearly that Jesus did not only use teaching to prepare the disciples to carry out the mission. Jesus modeled, healed the sick, demonstrated compassion, provided opportunities for on-the-job training, and critiqued their service. The disciples were readied to carry out the Great Commission quite possibly more by who Jesus was and what He did than by what He taught alone. Jesus was so confident of this varied approach to developing Christ-followers that He said to His disciples in John 14:12, "I tell you the truth, anyone who has faith in me will do what I have been doing. He will do even greater things than these" (NIV).

Gilbert Montez, small groups pastor at The Village Church in Highland Village, Texas, has taught me (Steve), "We believe that discipleship is everything we do, not something we sit down to do. Community, doing life together, and serving are keys to developing Christ-followers—because it is when we serve others we learn to love them and realize how much they really do matter to God."[1] That is precisely the reason developing Christ-followers with a servant's heart and evangelism are inseparable. Each is totally dependant upon the other.

The Local Church Is Still a Player

We continue to hold to the hope that the local church not only owns the responsibility of carrying out the Great Commission and must step up and accept its Christ-given call, but also that it can do this. No other entity in culture is in the business of changing hearts. The presence of the *ekklesia* in a community as a mission outpost[2] for the kingdom of God is the divine strategy to rescue people from the dominion of darkness (Col. 1:13). When a local fellowship of Christ-followers turns inward to perpetuate programs rather than serve in the name of Jesus, it has lost its *raison d'être* and is no longer of use for the reason Christ created it.

What are the essential elements of a local church? According to Frank Viola, a local church can be defined as "1. a plurality of people; 2. submission to the Headship of Christ; 3. a corporate meeting in a specific place."[3] A small group *or* a mega church can satisfy this description of a church, but a distinctive we acknowledge is that this plurality of people under the headship of Christ who meet corporately in a specific place must be about more than gathering to serve one another's needs. Jesus gave the authority of His name (Mt. 28:18) and the power of His Presence (Acts 1:8) to the church to complete its mission or "ministry of reconciliation" (2 Cor. 5:18). Just as the human persona *is*, it also *does*; and, so, the church *is* the "body of Christ," but it also *does* what Christ has co-missioned with it to accomplish as His Presence in the community.

Few would argue against the idea that the bride of Christ has been given the huge responsibility of fulfilling the Great Commandment and the Great Commission. Acts 2 is quite possibly the most often quoted chapter pertaining to the local church today. The passages provide a description of the attitudes, behaviors, and actions the first Christ-followers were displaying as they attempted to figure out how this church thing is supposed to work.

In some churches, developing Christ-followers has been hammered into a church program that may be accomplished through a small group ministry or a Sunday school organization. Other churches at the direction of their denomination have created a discipleship program that offers "studies" that people take to enhance their biblical knowledge of what it means to be a mature follower of Jesus. Materials are developed around the fives purposes of the church: evangelism, worship, discipleship, service, fellowship, and ministry.[4] The disciple, or, student, then takes a variety of courses (some in successive order) designed to teach the content and habits of a five-purpose lifestyle. The hopeful result is a disciple of Jesus, who knows and lives out the life described in the Bible. However, the opportunity to practice what one learns in these seminars and courses is typically not a part of the total experience. Some "homework" assignments offer suggestions for living out the newly ingested content, but seldom does actual mentoring or coaching take place outside the classroom.

CBSE is more than the church doing random acts of kindness or another disciple-making program. CBSE assists a Christ-follower to mature into the likeness of Christ by putting into practice the biblical truths, principles, and values he or she has learned by being a salt and light servant.

A Fellowship of Salt and Light Servants

We believe that the best way to live out Christ's teachings and examples as His disciples is as salt and light servants who exemplify the example and teachings of Jesus. His clearest words about the nature of leadership among His followers came after a "power play" by James and John. He concluded his leadership lesson with: "It [authority or power based leadership] is not this way among you, but whoever wishes to become great among you shall be your servant, and whoever wishes to be first among you shall be your slave; just as the Son of Man did not come to be served, but to serve, and to give His life a ransom for many" (Mt. 20:26–28; cf. Mk. 10:45). Christ-followers and churches must clearly understand their biblical role as servants who belong to Christ and influence others like salt and light in order to carry out the Great Commission in their communities. Otherwise, their attention will remain on themselves and their needs alone. Over forty years ago, Findley Edge wrote, "For this reason the church must always make sure that it sees and understands clearly its task in light of the spiritual purposes of God."[5] Those purposes include a servant's heart first toward God—who sent His Son to "buy" them for His own by His death, burial, and resurrection–and then toward others.

Living as a Fellowship of Servants

What does it mean to be a church that lives CBSE? Robert Lewis and Rob Wilkins state:

> Unless the church rediscovers its primary role as bridge builder, the incarnational power of the gospel will remain hidden, and the credibility necessary to reach a culture of cynical, experiential, and spiritually hungry souls will be lost. Even worse, the church's incomparable message of eternal and abundant life, despite relentless weekly proclamation, will continue to be largely ignored. People will simply no longer listen to or attend churches that seem incapable of living out what is preached. Bridges of influence–tangible and evident through the lifestyles and good works of believers–are the only answer.[6]

We agree with the authors that *bridges of influence–tangible and evident through the lifestyles and good works of believers–are the only answer* to impact a community in the name of Jesus. This happens when a fellowship of salt and light servants become aware of why God has planted them where they are and see that they are capable of building "bridges of influence" into the lives of those around them.

Remember the Old Testament story of Samuel? Eli, the boy's mentor, finally realized the voice in the night was that of the LORD, the God of Israel. He instructed the priest-in-training to answer, "Speak, for Your servant is listening" (1 Sam. 3:10). The next time he heard the voice, he did as his mentor taught him; and his life was never the same. We believe churches need to learn the voice of God again and answer as young Samuel did. Openness to God to accept His direction, no matter what the cost, is the first of the necessary elements for a Christ-follower to be a genuine servant and for the *ekklesia* to fulfill why Christ called it out to exist. The result of following Christ's command, being and acting like salt and light servants, is that the church begins to understand and apply the biblical truths, values, and principles it knows through knowing Christ.

Attitude is a church's second characteristic for becoming a fellowship of salt and light servants. Jesus is our example. Paul wrote to his friends in Philippi to have the same "attitude...which was also in Christ Jesus" (Phil. 2:5). He went on to describe that attitude: "But [Jesus] emptied Himself, taking the form of a bond-servant, and being made in the likeness of men…" (Phil. 2:7). Jesus laid aside His privileges of being God's Son to take the form of a bond-servant, or *doulos,* slave. We know that "the term 'servant' or 'bond slave' is often used by a man of God to describe his total dedication. Such submission to Christ is called in Romans 12:1 our 'reasonable service.'"[7]

Legacy Church, where Gene is senior pastor, has as one of their mottos, "God owns it. I manage it." A corollary to that value is that we live by "investing our time, talent, and treasures in people and projects that yield eternal value." In other words, we are God's investment managers, much like the house servant who managed his master's assets while he was away. Jesus told the parable of the talents to instruct His apprentices to be faithful in serving God with the talents, gifts, and abilities entrusted to them. Recall the master's pleasure when he returned and saw his servant (*doulos*) had increased his wealth through his work. Jesus completed His story by saying, "His master said to him, 'Well done, good and faithful [servant]. You have been faithful with a few things; I will put you in charge of many things. Come and share your master's happiness!'" (Mt. 25:21, NIV). For twenty-one centuries, Christ-followers and churches have been motivated with the promise of hearing these words upon entering heaven.

Serving in Christ's name enables an individual to have an attitude similar to Christ's. The attitude of a devoted follower of Christ assists the Christian in developing a salt and light servant lifestyle. Growing in the skills and ways of Jesus while serving with a servant's heart are key to being a holy presence in one's community. The two are inseparably connected.

Developing Salt and Light Servants

Prior to a discussion on how intentional development of salt and light servants can positively influence your church's effectiveness in reaching those far from God, we must first describe the end picture or "product" we are seeking to produce by our work as servant leaders in the mission of Christ.

Churches typically have neglected to leverage service and evangelism as tools to assist their people to become devoted followers of Christ. Our churches are full of individuals who have bought into the old paradigm of attendance in worship and Bible studies as adequate preparation to form a Christlike life.

The new paradigm requires the Christ-follower to serve in Kingdom endeavors. Gene Mims wrote, "Kingdom means the reign of God in the lives of His people, enabling them to serve Him wholeheartedly and to live the kind of life Jesus died to give us. It is His Holy Spirit working in us, through us, and around us in such a way that we actually live and do the will of God."[8]

Therefore, to see people come into relationship with Christ, Christ-followers are to be on mission and engaged serving those in the community, as did Jesus. Mims continues:

> Life in the kingdom of God is not a sheltered, careful life without risk, failure, achievement, or excitement. It's a life that's real in that everything we face is real. Life is filled with good and bad. We have joy alongside out sorrows and triumphs along with our defeats. Kingdom living is not an escape. It is engagement. It is living at the highest human level even in the midst of the lowest human experience.[9]

The process of helping members understand that worship and Bible study are important, but, by themselves, are not adequate to form Christ in them, will be a difficult change for many. After all, it is easy to come to church on a Sunday morning for Sunday school and worship. It takes more effort to love others as Jesus did the other six days of the week. Additionally, many have never been exposed to the possibility that they can develop their relationship with Christ at the same time they are coaching a little league team and giving a reason for what they believe to their players and the players' parents.

This shift in focus will take time and multiple experiences for individuals to understand, grasp, and act out. However, when the church is released into the community as salt and light servants, the spiritual maturity level in a local church cannot help but rise. A radical change is necessary because our processes simply are not producing the desired results. We have tried quick fixes and minor changes, placing bandages on church programs, ministries, and events. The results have been at best minimal. Frank Viola concludes, "True renewal, therefore, must be radical. That means it must go to the root! Recovering the Lord's testimony necessitates that we forsake our ecclesiastical patches and band-aids!"[10]

In my (Gene's) study, *Paul on Leadership*, I ask the church that is considering the leap from functioning as a typical "local church" to a "mission outpost," like the *ekklesia* in Antioch (Acts 11) to answer five groups of questions that test its readiness for change. We include them here for your consideration.

Five Questions Your Church Must Answer

1. Why has God placed us in this mission field? The answer to this question is your purpose or mission.

2. If we say we know why we are here, is everything we do currently contributing to that reason for being or mission? If so, how are we enhancing that ministry's effectiveness? If not, are we willing to change or remove those things that are not contributing to our mission? The answers to these questions guide your initial decisions for change.

3. What is God's picture of what we should become? Can we paint that picture in twenty-five words or less, or in a drawing or picture? The answers to these questions provide a simple picture of your future. This God-inspired image is what you transition toward.

4. Has the core leadership prayerfully accepted the mission as God's call on the church body as a whole? If so, are they willing to put into practice the implications of that call? If not, what issues need to be addressed before there is agreement about the implications of the call? The answers to these questions will help you discover who will be the leaders of the transition and those you need to continue to serve as you lead them into God's future for your church.

5. What essential changes do we need to make to become what God has called us to be? The answers to this question begin the detailed process of strategic decision-making to become what God has called you to do and become.

We believe churches can make the necessary changes to create a fellowship of salt and light servants who impact their mission fields in the name of Jesus.

Service Is the Path to Impacting Your Community

Serving will assist Christ-followers in their personal spiritual development. Serving can do what worship, Bible study, and or even sharing one's faith cannot. Scripture is full of passages that implore Jesus' disciples to live lives of service. One example is Paul's passionate reminder to the Christians in Galatia, "For you were called to freedom, brethren; only do not turn your freedom into an opportunity for the flesh, but through love serve (*douleuete*) one another" (Gal. 5:13). The authors of *Network* remind us: "The word 'serve' is a command. That means serving for the believer is not an option. Most of us know we should serve. And most of us really want to serve. But many of us are just not sure how we can serve in a way that makes us fruitful and fulfilled."[11] Members genuinely desire to engage in Kingdom business. They want to know their gift of service is making a difference and is contributing toward Kingdom advancement. This reality calls each of us in church leadership to answer an important question: "What are the ways our members contribute to Kingdom advancement?" Service also allows Christ-followers to glorify God. Service is worship. We can and do worship our Lord when we serve people. Scripture implores us, "Whoever speaks, is to do so as one who is speaking the utterances of God; whoever serves (*diakonei*) is to do so as one who is serving by the strength which God supplies; so that in all things God may be glorified through Jesus Christ, to whom belongs the glory and dominion forever and ever. Amen" (1 Pet. 4:11). Jesus called for His apprentices to "let your light shine...that they may see your good works, and glorify (*doxasosai*) your Father who is in heaven" (Mt. 5:16). To serve is to shine the light of God's love on others, and in doing so, bring honor and fame to the One who served us first.

Jesus knew that for those who answered His call to follow him to become fully devoted to Him they must live like salt and light servants. Service is a key to developing our personal relationship with Him. Edge punctuates this truth: "Growth is not optional for one who is in Christ!"[12] Churches carry the responsibility to develop this servant-oriented growth among their members. Dallas Willard insightfully stated:

> The way to get as many people into heaven as you can is to get heaven into as many people as you can—that is, to follow the path of genuine spiritual transformation or full-throttle discipleship to Christ. When we are counting up results, we also need to keep in mind the multitudes of people who will not be in heaven because they have never, to their knowledge, seen the reality of Christ in a living human being.[13]

Service is one way in which the "multitudes of people" see the "reality of Christ in a living human being." Pietistic displays of "holier than thou" attitudes will keep those Christ died for at a distance. Serving in the name of Jesus builds bridges of influence to live out the witness we are in Christ. Wayne Cordeiro declares, "You see, God is less interested in what you are doing and much more interested in what you're becoming."[14] If you are becoming a Christlike servant of God, you will do those things that God will use to draw people to Him.

What Am I to Become?

The second part of the Great Commission—that is, equipping—is as crucial for the individual and the *ekklesia* as the reaching aspect of our co-mission with Christ. To equip people for service in the name of Jesus is to demonstrate the love of God that indwells us and compels us to love others. Steve Ayers observes, "The grace of God is activated as we reach out to others, serve others, and lift others up. We activate grace when we honor God. Serve others, for by this, people will know that you love God."[15] Rusaw and Swanson concur: "Nearly everything that is done inside the church should prepare and equip people not only for personal growth but also for personal impact."[16] "Teaching" as found in the Great Commission must be more like Jesus' training of the Twelve than like our enlightened teaching of the multitudes. Equip people to serve, and they will learn by doing rather than by schooling.

Churches for years have sought to assist people to become Christlike without ever taking the time to *describe* what it is to be Christlike. It may help if we take the time to provide a portrait for our members to see. What is a salt and light servant, or follower of Jesus? What do they do? How do they act? What are their attitudes? Randy Pope, pastor of Perimeter Church in Atlanta, Georgia, describes a mature and equipped follower of Christ as one who:

- lives consistently under the control of the Holy Spirit, the direction of the word of God, and the compelling love of Christ
- has discovered, developed, and is using his or her spiritual gifts
- has learned to effectively share his or her faith while demonstrating radical love that amazes the world that it touches
- gives strong evidence of being a faithful member of God's church
- is an effective manager of life, relationships, and resources
- is a willing minister to God's people
- is available when needed for ministry
- demonstrates a life characterized as gospel driven, worship focused morally pure, evangelistically bold, discipleship grounded, family faithful socially responsible.[17]

These characteristics of a salt and light servant do not come as a result of sitting and hearing a preacher/teacher week after week. Pope's portrait of a mature and equipped Christ-follower includes actions and behaviors that show evidence of a heart captured by the love of God.

Jesus engaged the real needs of people to demonstrate the love of the Father and as a sign of who He was. His acts of service include His encounter with the Samaritan woman (Jn. 4), Zaccheus (Lk. 19), the criminal crucified beside Jesus (Lk. 23), and the 5000 people He miraculously fed (Mt.14).

The disciple Matthew demonstrated Kingdom service when, shortly after his encounter with Christ, he invited the other disciples and his tax-collecting buddies to his home. He was untrained in "evangelism," and he threw his party very soon after his "yes" to follow Jesus. (Maybe we don't need to make people feel as if they must go through "class" before they begin to tell their friends about their newly found hope in Christ?) Matthew invited his friends to his party to connect Jesus with them. For the connection to take place, Matthew had to serve Jesus, the other disciples, and Matthew's friends someplace other than the local place of worship, the synagogue, where "those kinds of people" were not allowed. The most natural and spiritually neutral place was his home.

The local religious leaders dropped by to check things out. When they saw what was going on, they accused Jesus of eating and drinking with "tax-gathers" and "sinners," technical religious terms that excluded those people from the culture created by the religious elite. Jesus responded to their elitist attitude by making His mission statement known: "It is not those who are well who need a physician, but those who are sick. I have not come to call the righteous but sinners to repentance" (Lk. 5:31–32). Matthew not only connected his friends with Jesus through his act of service, but he also gave the religious leaders an opportunity to encounter the Sent One.

In the same manner, as Jesus served people throughout His earthly ministry, churches and Christ-followers must also serve those far from God today. Serving is absolutely vital to the fulfillment of both halves of the Great Commission. Churches must look at the life of Christ and take notice of how He intentionally leveraged every opportunity to share with the people how much people matter to God. In the process, churches today must overcome many obstacles to fulfill the Great Commission. For example, one common perception among those in your community is, "Six out of ten Americans believe the church is irrelevant. Rarely is the church mentioned publicly as being an asset to our area by anyone. We are generally ignored by community leaders and often left out of community life."[18] Robert Lewis, pastor of Little Rock's Fellowship Bible Church, found that as he researched the community, people actually were looking for a church to be more involved in the community. Lewis also discovered that the residents of Little Rock were confused as to why churches were disengaged with the greater Little Rock community. The local church must hear Jesus' words: "Behold, I say to you, lift up your eyes and look on the fields, that they are white for harvest" (Jn. 4:35b).

The following quote by Randy Pope should be read multiple times. It is so different from how many of our churches operate that it will take multiple readings for the truth of the statement to thoroughly soak in. "Much in the way that eating creates no appetite for exercise, so, too, I have found that Bible study and prayer alone do not create mission-oriented Christians. But, just as exercise creates a desire for food and drink, mission-related activities create an insatiable thirst and hunger to feed on God's Word."[19]

We (the authors) both run marathons. Don't ask us why we do it, but there is something about the challenge of pushing your body beyond its normal capacities and accomplishing something only about .1 percent of the population will ever experience that drives us to do this. Eating has never created in us a desire to exercise, but preparing to run 26.2 miles in about four hours definitely creates not only a desire but a need to eat. Yes, diet is crucial to one's overall performance, but exercise produces a desire for food. Food, on the other hand, especially ice cream, has never motivated me to get up and train–actually, the sugar de-motivates me to do what is required to finish the race well.

Could it possibly be that simple? Could service really be the missing, motivating factor in developing fully devoted followers of Christ? It is important for church leaders to understand, along with John Ortberg, "Information alone does not transform the human heart and character. In order for a spiritual transformation to take place, certain action and experiences are required."[20] What would happen if your goal became the number of people involved in community service rather than in Bible Study? What if your emphasis became serving in the name of Jesus rather than learning in the classroom? We contend that just as you need both exercise and diet to be an effective long-distance runner, so Jesus' apprentices should be engaged in both serving and learning–but with the caveat that serving will motivate learning, not the other way around.

How comfortable are you with this manner of thinking? If you adopted the truth of Pope's observation, what would you need to adjust and or change to be a church that seeks to involve every member in Christlike service for the purpose of telling the Good News? Where would you look for opportunities to serve outside the church's organizational chart? Who could you contact in the community to partner with to meet a community need?

We endorse Rick Warren's "Purpose Driven" *40 Days of Community*[21] as an effective way to build community within the church while mobilizing people to meet a community need. Warren's way is a healthy combination of gathering and sending that can impact the mission field in which you find yourself while building up the fellowship of the church. Gene has seen the power of this campaign in his own church as they partnered with the school district to serve unwed student mothers in their city.

Spiritual Maturity Inventory

A unique tool we have developed is the "Spiritual Maturity Inventory" found in appendix 1, available for download at www. chalicepress.com. It is a tool to assist you and your church to know where each individual stands in his or her personal relationship with Christ. The Spiritual Maturity Inventory is provided as a tool for every member, regular attender, and guest to encounter the verses in the New Testament descriptive of what a Christ-follower is to become. The inventory uses Scripture for its base and has as its foundational belief, "The word of God is...sharper than any two-edged sword" (Heb. 4:12a). The commonly held five functions of a local church provide the framework for maturity and are the categories for the individual utilizing this tool.

You may ask, "How does this Spiritual Maturity Inventory help address great commandment evangelism?" The five purposes of a person's life in Christ have become a biblical norm of balance and maturity for many who have said yes to God's call and apprenticed themselves to Jesus. The "five G's" as described by Willow Creek Community Church–Grace, Growth, Groups, Gifts, and Good stewardship–form a path for life-long spiritual formation.[22] Steve has developed the Spiritual Maturity Inventory around the five purposes of spiritual vitality in one who follows Jesus. Serving alone is as much of a sign of imbalance as study alone. This inventory aids the follower of Christ to evaluate him- or herself against the biblical descriptions of a vital Christian life.

We offer this inventory because we also believe that loving God is an ongoing process. Our love for Him today should be greater than it was yesterday. Our love for Him compels us to love others. Second, our love for others assists us in loving God. Third, developing one's personal love relationship with Christ is inseparable from evangelism. If we truly love Him, we are engaged in telling others about Him. Fourth, one's personal relationship with Christ along with current stories of how He is working in our lives are what provide us with the best tool in leading others into beginning a relationship with Christ.

Fifth, we believe Christ-followers cannot consider themselves devoted followers unless they are actively involved sharing with people far from God. Nowhere in Scripture can a Christian find support for taking a pass on being involved in evangelism. The fruit of a Christ-follower is another Christ-follower. After all, it was Jesus who said, "You will know them by their fruits" (Mt. 7:20).

Finally, the Great Commission includes the word *and*. Go "and" make. In the same way, we cannot separate loving God and loving others, we cannot separate going and making. They are dependent upon each other.

The Spiritual Maturity Inventory will help you and your church see where you currently place your emphasis or spend most of your time, effort, and money developing salt and light servants. We predict that more church members will find a deficit in service–"Good Stewardship"–than in Growth or other characteristics. If this is the case, CBSE can be a way to balance your approach to equipping members as missionaries in their mission field of the community.

QUESTIONS FOR DISCUSSION

1. What options does your church provide for members and regular attenders to develop into "salt and light servants"? What percentage of time and resources are allocated to:

   _____ Bible study courses
   _____ Small groups
   _____ Service
   _____ Evangelism

2. Accomplishing the Great Commandment and the Great Commission *requires a church to be open to God's direction.* Is your church open? Why or why not? What steps do we need to take?

3. Re-address the following questions:

   • Why has God placed us in this mission field?
   • If we say we know why we are here, is everything we do currently contributing to that reason for being or mission? If so, how are we enhancing that ministry's effectiveness? If not, are we willing to change or remove those things that are not contributing to our mission?
   • What is God's picture of what we should become? Can we paint that picture in twenty-five words or less or in a drawing or picture?

- Has the core leadership prayerfully accepted the mission as God's call on the church body as a whole? If so, are they willing to put into practice the implications of that call? If not, what issues need to be addressed before there is agreement about the implications of the call?
- What essential changes do we need to make to become what God has called us to be?

4. Have you specifically defined what you are attempting to assist people to become?

Notes

[1]Personal conversation with Gilbert Montez.

[2]C. Gene Wilkes, *Paul on Leadership: Servant Leadership in a Ministry of Transition* (Nashville: LifeWay, 2004), 58.

[3]Frank Viola, *Rethinking the Wineskin* (Gainesville: Present Testimony Ministry, 2001), 136.

[4]Rick Warren, *The Purpose Driven Church* (Grand Rapids: Zondervan, 1995).

[5]Findley B. Edge, *A Quest for Vitality in Religion* (Nashville: Broadman Press, 1963), 69.

[6]Robert Lewis and Rob Wilkins, *The Church of Irresistible Influence* (Grand Rapids: Zondervan, 2001), 177.

[7]Charles F. Pfeiffer, Howard F. Vos, John Rea, eds., *Wycliffe Bible Encyclopedia*, vol. 2 (Chicago: Moody Press, The Moody Bible Institute of Chicago, 1975), 1556.

[8]Gene Mims, *The Kingdom Focused Church* (Nashville: Broadman and Holman, 2003), 40.

[9]Ibid., 41.

[10]Viola, *Rethinking the Wineskin*, 79.

[11]Bruce Bugbee, Don Cousins, and Bill Hybels, *Network: Leaders Guide* (Grand Rapids: Zondervan, 1994), 34.

[12]Edge, *Quest for Vitality*, 91.

[13]Dallas Willard, *Renovation of the Heart* (Colorado Springs: NavPress, 2002), 239.

[14]Wayne Cordeiro, *Doing Church as a Team* (Honolulu: New Hope Publishing, 1998), 133.

[15]Steve Ayers, *Igniting Passion in Your Church* (Loveland: Group Publishing, 2003), 116.

[16]Rick Rusaw and Eric Swanson, *The Externally Focused Church* (Loveland: Group Publishing, 2004), 17–18.

[17]Randy Pope, *The Prevailing Church* (Chicago: Moody Press, 2002), 84–85.

[18]Lewis and Wilkins, *Church of Irresistible Influence*, 23, 196.

[19]Pope, *Prevailing Church*, 34.

[20]John Ortberg, *If You Want to Walk on Water, You've Got to Get Out of the Boat* (Grand Rapids: Zondervan, 2001), 79.

[21]Go to www.purposedriven.com and click on "Campaigns" to read about the details of "40 Days of Community."

[22]Go to www.willowcreek.org and click on "Growth" and "Membership" and then "Five G's" to find the details and materials that support this concept of spiritual formation.

6

Connection Points

Community-Based Evangelism *Training*

In the spring of 2007, the city of Denton suffered through a flash flood. Thankfully, no one was killed or seriously injured; however, a great deal of private and community property was damaged. Calhoun Middle School suffered serious water damage. The Village Church, Denton campus, is located less than two blocks away from Calhoun. The response was "organic." The Village Church, Denton Campus, provided volunteers to clean and paint the school. This resulted in a close relationship and trust being developed between school teachers, district officials, and The Village Church and a lasting opportunity to be "salt and light."

Having now trained thousands of people in how to share their faith, I (Steve) often have wondered what has been the result of my personal investment and that of the seminar participants. Even if only a fraction of those attending the seminars were to actually share their faith, the "numbers" should begin reflecting a positive upturn. However, after comparing the numbers of church members in a particular church prior to the seminar with those the year following, only the rare church has an increase of more than five conversions over the prior year.

So a small change was made in the teaching of the seminar. Recently I have begun to encourage those at the seminars to alter how they do life if they are going to connect with people far from God. I now encourage everyone, for one month, to make a slight change in how they might purchase items at stores. I suggest they not pay at the pump or check themselves out of grocery and discount stores. This simple change in behavior results in countless opportunities for connection. This encourages them to meet and interact with someone to whom odds are they could "give a reason for what they believe."

I realize the majority of the seminar participants will not follow through on my challenge. However, Denise from a church in Oklahoma did. On the way home after the evangelism seminar, Denise stopped by the gas station. She said she started to pay at the pump, but at the last minute remembered my challenge. She went in and handed the clerk her credit card, pumped her gas, and returned to sign the receipt. As she reentered the store, she observed that the young woman was crying. She immediately thought, "Oh no, I might have just put myself in a position with which I am not going to be comfortable."

She shared that no one else was in the store. She had several other responsibilities to take care of before heading home; however, she pushed the pause button and asked what was wrong and was there anything she could do? The young girl shared that one of her best friends was just in a serious car accident. Denise asked her if she would like her to pray for her friend. The clerk's response was, "What? Right here, right now?" Denise responded, "Yes, we don't have to be in a church to pray." The prayer Denise said that day began a relationship with Sara, the clerk. Six months later, it resulted in Sara beginning a relationship with Christ.

It may not surprise you that Denise discovered she had the spiritual gift of evangelism. Since that day, she has led nearly twenty people into personal relationships with Christ over a three-year period. It comes naturally to her. If she connects with a person far from God, a sixth sense takes over. She just knows how to leverage the connection with the individual to a relationship with Christ. But, for those of us who do not have the spiritual gift of evangelism, taking people from a connection point to a personal relationship with Christ does not come quite as easy.

Churches are beginning to ask, "Why is it that training people how to share their faith in most cases does not result in new Christ-followers?" Is there the proverbial "missing ingredient" that must be added? What needs to be included that is currently not a part of any of the evangelism training courses? Could some of our teaching points actually be *causing* some of the issues?

Intentionally re-engaging the culture is something we have done in addition to serving full-time in ministry positions. Steve has coached little league baseball, football, and soccer, served as the president of two homeowner associations, and served as a member of the economic development committee of the city of Wheat Ridge, Colorado. Gene has served as a volunteer Police and Fire Department Chaplain and as a member of the school district's Diversity Advocacy Committee. Gene has become a member of two running groups and a cycling group to find connection points with those far from God. Every time we have volunteered or joined an interest group, God has used our connection with people far from God to lead at least one person into a personal relationship with Christ.

To fulfill the front half of the Great Commission, the process will always begin with a Christ-follower connecting with someone far from God. To lead someone into a personal relationship with Christ has little to do with whether someone has attended training and learned a model presentation of the gospel.

While we are on this point, an additional statement needs to be made. Could the real issue actually not be, "How do we train our members on how to share their faith?" Is the chief issue that our people have nothing to share regarding what Jesus is actually doing in their lives? If Jesus is active and the personal relationship is growing, there is no doubt about it—we *will* have something to share. The real problem is many people in our churches do not have a vibrant relationship with Christ.

Connection Points

How to Find Connection Points

"My daughter's pregnant," my friend said on the other end of the phone. I mumbled something, and he continued. "Yes, we're certain. I need to talk to you." That's how our (Gene's) church became connected to the local school district's program to help school-aged parents graduate from high school and meet their needs in the process. The fifteen-year-old daughter of my friend joined the school district program to stay in school as she prepared to give birth to her baby. That experience became a connection point to serve the school-aged parents in our community.

Our church came around the family to support their daughter's decision to keep the baby and in doing so we discovered opportunities to serve the needs of other girls and their families. We teamed with other churches and organizations to provide everything from infant formula to car seats, and sponsored the meals and volunteers for the monthly meetings the director holds for the girls, the fathers, and their families during the school year. We initially hosted a baby shower for the family in our church, and then we hosted a church-wide shower to stock the resource center in the school-aged parent program.

This connection point also allowed partnerships with two of our existing community-based ministries: a pregnancy resource center and a transformational housing ministry for homeless women. The network of resources in place now provide connection points from abstinence training to transforming the lives of homeless women and their children in the name of Jesus.

A mistimed choice that caused a pregnancy provided a connection point to serve that family and the network of relationships that the experience created.

The first step in assisting church members to become engaged in evangelism is not training, but ensuring that they have growing, developing, and maturing personal relationships with Christ. We know of no other way to accomplish this first step than to utilize small groups. Small groups provide an accountability ingredient to develop a personal relationship with Christ.

Connection point possibilities surround us each and every day. Churches should take every opportunity available to them to encourage and assist their members in finding connection points in their communities. Many times, we are blind to the reality of a possible connection point. Sometimes, we can see a possibility but choose not to act. It is our perception of the situation that drives the decision—whether we will act or not. "We humans could help by creating the healthy environments in which people naturally connect. If we would concentrate upon facilitating the environment instead of the result (people experiencing community), we might see healthy, spontaneous community emerge."[1] Therefore, the key is not just being able to perceive the possibility, but also to act. Churches can assist members in creating a context for connecting, but it is up to the individual whether to act on the connection or not. Therefore, *the second key* in organically developing people to become engaged in evangelism is noticing the connection points we have each and every day and doing something with them.

A *third potential connection point* is with people we have known or who are already in our network of relationships. The authors of *Becoming a Contagious Christian* give us three connection point possibilities: people we already know, people we used to know, and people we would like to know.[2] The *people we already know* would be our family members, neighbors, friends, and acquaintances. A connection point has already been made and currently exists with this type of person. We may or may not have similar interests or hobbies, but we already have some degree of relationship. Giving a reason for what you believe, loving and caring, and including them in activities you are already doing, have the strong possibility of the person beginning a relationship with Christ.

The second type of person, *people we used to know,* includes individuals we had relationships with in the past. Those in this category would be our neighbors who moved across town, people with whom we used to attend school with, people who worked in the same office, and people who were friends with our children. Once again, connection has previously taken place, and the key becomes building on the past relationship. We should be quick to note that, even though a prior relationship existed, there may or may not be similar interests. This type of connection will need to be rekindled slowly, leveraging the past to build on a possible future.

A connection point with *people we would like to know* is more easily developed if we have a prior inherent interest or desire. It may be who they are, but, more likely, it is what they do that becomes the connection point. Developing this bridge with someone we would like to know occurs best through interests or passion. Passion has the ability to assist us to where we might settle in serving.

Perhaps an example might be helpful. Let's say my passion is children. My interest is sports. My spiritual gifts are administration, teaching, and leadership. My son needs a little league coach. At his insistence, I accept the managerial position.

In addition to a thorough knowledge and understanding of the sport, a successful coach needs not only to know his or her players' strengths and weaknesses, but also the players' parents. Baseball is a team sport. As far as little league goes, the team is composed of all the children and all the parents. Immediately, I have at least nine connection point possibilities. At these connection point relationships can be developed. As a Christ-follower, my heart's desire then is for them to ask me for the reason for my faith. Therefore, the key evangelism question for churches is not how we can train everyone in how to share their faith–the key question is, "How can I build that connection point(s) into an authentic relationship?"

We have come to realize that not assisting our church members to develop a connection point into an authentic relationship is simply not providing good leadership. Our lack of leading in this area will cause many to miss the opportunities that God has placed before them. Developing connection can no longer be left to chance. Connection points and how to develop them must be taught and modeled if we are to fulfill the Great Commandment and Great Commission. Doug Pagitt and Tony Jones observe, "Our theological engagement and concerns ought to be developed from the questions and needs of the world around us. Far too long, we have gone out into the world to tell people what we think they ought to know rather than seeking to discover what they are interested in and where they are looking for answers."[3]

The old way to develop relationships would be to go to dinner, to a movie, a backyard barbeque, or some similar activity. Spending time together is critical to developing a new relationship. The relationship must have the possibility for additional depth. Relationships develop best around a need the mutual relationship can meet.

We are now ready to move to the *fourth organic key*: How can we leverage the individual's needs in developing our relationship to the point the person wants to know our spiritual story? Ron Lewis taught the importance of connecting the gospel message to America's felt needs. Therefore, if we as Christ's ambassadors can meet someone's felt needs, we have a greater possibility of developing the relationship to the point to which we will have the opportunity of giving the reason for our faith. "Christ went to where the broken, sick, and sinful people could be found. He did not demand their repentance before He spent time with them."[4] According to Ron, America's top five felt needs are loneliness, hopelessness, purposelessness, emptiness, and fear. Felt needs provide a handle to develop a connection point into an authentic relationship with people far from God.

The discussion of the five top felt needs is our way of training Christ-followers in how to share their faith in an organic fashion. The felt needs can either be taught on a Sunday morning or become the focal biblical passages for children, students, and adults in their small groups. Additionally, every time the Sunday teaching or small group material is on an encounter Jesus had with someone, the felt need Jesus leveraged can be mentioned. Keeping the key point of leveraging felt needs on the front burner can potentially make an eternal different in many people's lives.

In the following pages, we will focus on the five felt needs and how Jesus leveraged the individual's need to transform that person's life. We all know that narratives have the ability to touch a person in an emotional fashion. Stories can and do transform a person's perspective in life. There was and is no one better than Jesus Himself to teach us today on how to connect organically with a need.

Organic Evangelism Training

Loneliness: Zaccheus (Lk. 19:1–10)

With all the technological advancements, it is difficult initially to understand why loneliness is one of American's top felt needs. Cell phones can keep us connected wherever we are. Computers provide opportunities to connect though e-mail and instant messenger. Automobiles and air travel allow us to keep connected with family and friends. But, the problem is, this all only allows for connection. A connection does not always equal relationship. Such connections, in fact, turn out to be poor substitutes for relationship. Or they become the means by which we postpone developing relationships. Something deeper must be a part of the connection to allow it to develop. Meeting the human need of loneliness can be the tracks on which we can journey to authentic relationship. Ray Oldenburg states, "As many an urbanite and suburbanite has learned, having an extensive network of friends is no guarantee against loneliness. Nor does membership in voluntary associations, the 'instant communities' of our mobile society, ensure against social isolation and attendant feelings of boredom and alienation. What urban life increasingly fails to provide—what is so much missed—is convenient and open-ended socializing, places where individuals can go without aim or arrangement and be greeted by people who know them and know how to enjoy a little time off."[5] In His public ministry, Jesus noticed many lonely people. Some were even in a crowd. He gave us examples of how to leverage loneliness to develop an authentic relationship. Many of the people Jesus healed were lonely. The stories of the blind man, the woman at the well, the adulterous woman, and the prodigal son all contain some level of loneliness. The story of Zaccheus, the Jewish tax collector, possibly gives us the best insight into how to leverage loneliness. In Luke 19, we find the encounter:

> He entered Jericho and was passing through. And there was a man called by the name of Zaccheus; he was a chief tax collector and he was rich. Zaccheus was trying to see who Jesus was, and was unable because of the crowd, for he was small in stature. So he ran on ahead and climbed up into a sycamore tree in order to see Him, for He was about to pass through that way. When Jesus came to the place, He looked up and said to him, "Zaccheus, hurry and come down, for today I must stay at your house." And he hurried and came down and received Him gladly. When they saw it, they all began to grumble, saying, "He has gone to be the guest of a man who is a sinner." Zaccheus stopped and said to the Lord,

"Behold Lord, half of my possessions I will give to the poor, and if I have defrauded anyone of anything, I will give back four times as much." And Jesus said to him, "Today salvation has come to this house, because he, too, is a son of Abraham. For the Son of Man has come to seek and to save that which was lost." (Lk. 19:1–10)

Loneliness oozes throughout this story. Jesus gives us five handles on how to leverage loneliness to build relationships.

Further unpacking the context, Zaccheus was alone. You may say it does not take much brainpower to come up with this point, but this is possibly the most critical aspect of the encounter. Both the Jews and the Romans despised Jewish tax collectors. If someone chose this profession, wealth would most likely be the goal. This choice would exact a huge price. Zaccheus would have to journey through life without a best friend. He could afford house servants, and possibly at one time thought he could buy friendships. Sadly, at this most exciting time in his life, Zaccheus had no one with whom to share the moment.

First, *Jesus noticed.* He was observant. He identified the person first. Jesus probably noticed a small man trying to get an eye on Him. He saw him run ahead and climb up a tree. He is a Jewish tax collector, a very wealthy man, dressed to the hilt, not only running but also soiling his garments struggling to climb a tree. Jesus immediately recognized an opportunity to share real life with him.

Second, as my friend Mark Mittelberg would say, *Jesus did not do a drive-by conversion.* The Son of God, who came to seek and to save that which was lost (Lk. 19:10), chose to push the pause button on His journey and spend quality time with a lonely man. Jesus saw how Zaccheus's loneliness could be leveraged to change where he was going to spend eternity. Jesus knew a Bible study, a confrontational presentation of the gospel message, or preaching on the street corner did not have as strong a possibility as would having dinner with him at his house.

Third, *Jesus stayed focused on Zaccheus.* Jesus was so focused on Zaccheus that it did not matter to Him that the religious folks were upset because he was hanging out with a sinner. Jesus' focus was Zaccheus and where he was going to spend eternity. That was far more important to Jesus than any criticism and name calling by the Pharisees and scribes. Jesus, taking the heat for hanging out with a sinner, demonstrated to Zaccheus how much he really mattered. Jesus loved the title "friend of sinners." As Christ-followers, we must not be afraid of being called the same.

Fourth, *Jesus gave Zaccheus permission to demonstrate his life change.* After spending some time with Jesus, Zaccheus decided he must give half of his possessions to the poor and pay any person he had defrauded four times as much. By listening and encouraging him to make such a commitment, Jesus helped Zaccheus to understand the life change that took place.

Finally, *Jesus shared with Zaccheus why He took time out from His journey.* Jesus, in fact, shared His personal mission statement with Zaccheus in his house that day: "For the Son of Man has come to seek and to save that which was lost" (Luke 19:10). To put loneliness behind us once and for all, we must connect to something larger than ourselves. Jesus' vision to change the world was the vision to which Zaccheus found himself connected. By passing on the mission, Jesus immediately made Zaccheus a missionary to the lonely. Zaccheus clearly understood how painful loneliness was. Jesus immediately commissioned him into action to change the trajectory of people he would really like to know.

As we make connection in our communities with people far from God, we need to be sensitive to this heartfelt need. Loneliness can motivate people to do things that they might not ever consider. Jesus leveraged loneliness to change the eternal destination of Zaccheus. As His followers today, we must be sensitive to individuals demonstrating this felt need and pursue them with the same bulldog-like tenacity as Jesus.

Do we know people like Zaccheus–folks who are extremely lonely? Could it be that we need to take the time–as Jesus did–to leverage the opportunities that come our way to connect with and begin building relationships with such people?

Mark called one day and said he needed to talk with me (Gene). We were good friends, and his request was not unusual. We met at our usual coffee shop (a "third place" for us). He had recently gone through a yearlong coaching program at work that resulted in a visit to a major U.S. city to see a ministry his grandfather supported. There he saw a housing ministry for battered women that he could not shake from his heart. After he told me the details of what he had seen, he told me he felt he had to do this in Dallas. I'm never one to discourage a God-sized vision, so, I said I would pray and support him and Legacy Church would provide whatever we could to help.

That was in 2002. In the fall of 2007 there are two homes in the Dallas area with graduates of the two-year, highly supervised, faith-based training program who have college associate degrees, jobs, and are living on their own. Each resident is required not only to complete the practical training but also to attend a local church during her residency. Legacy Church is the local fellowship for the home in Plano, and we have been able to partner with Mark and his ministry in many ways. Several women have found not only a new life off the streets, but also a new life in Christ! Dallas Providence Homes, Inc., has a goal of ten houses in the Dallas area by 2010 and ultimately "to have at least one Providence Home in every major U.S. city" by 2015.[6] Look for one in your city soon!

Some connection points rise up from among the church's membership when they see their "ministry" is not just within the walls of the buildings, but wherever God leads them. We did not put a strategy planning committee together to find ministries in our community. God had already chosen one from among those who were the *ekklesia* called Legacy.

Hopelessness: The Demoniac Cured (Lk. 8:26–39)

Then they sailed to the country of the Gerasenes, which is opposite Galilee. And when He came out onto the land, He was met by a man from the city who was possessed with demons; and who had not put on any clothing for a long time, and was not living in a house, but in the tombs. Seeing Jesus, he cried out and fell before Him, and said in a loud voice, "What business do we have with each other, Jesus, Son of the Most High God? I beg You, do not torment me." For He had commanded the unclean spirit to come out of the man. For it had seized him many times; and he was bound with chains and shackles and kept under guard, and yet he would break his bonds and be driven by the demon into the desert. And Jesus asked him, "What is your name?" And he said, "Legion"; for many demons had entered him. They were imploring Him not to command them to go away into the abyss. Now there was a herd of many swine feeding there on the mountain; and the demons implored Him to permit them to enter the swine. And He gave them permission. And the demons came out of the man and entered the swine; and the herd rushed down the steep bank into the lake and was drowned. When the herdsmen saw what had happened, they ran away and reported it in the city and out in the country. The people went out to see what had happened; and they came to Jesus, and found the man from whom the demons had gone out, sitting down at the feet of Jesus, clothed and in his right mind; and they became frightened. Those who had seen it reported to them how the man who was demon-possessed had been made well. And all the people of the country of the Gerasenes and the surrounding district asked Him to leave them, for they were gripped with great fear; and He got into a boat and returned. But the man from whom the demons had gone out was begging Him that he might accompany Him; but He sent him away, saying, "Return to your house and describe what great things God has done for you." So he went away, proclaiming throughout the whole city what great things Jesus had done for him.

Only a few men live in a more hopeless state than that of Legion. Evidently, for years he had terrorized people in Gerasene. The Bible describes Legion as a man possessed by demons and able to break chains that were used to attempt confinement. Jesus gives us a lesson on how to deal effectively with a person who is desperately hopeless.

First, *Jesus allowed and possibly encouraged Legion to approach.* Jesus did not cower; He did not back away. He opened wide His arms and encouraged him to come. The Bible says that Legion came all the way up and fell at Jesus' feet. The only other people Legion had come into close proximity with were those who were attempting to confine him by chains. Jesus did not come with chains, but with open arms and a welcoming expression. For years, Legion had experienced only disgust, fear, revulsion, shock, and hatred. Instead, Jesus showed Legion compassion. For the first time in years, Legion felt he really mattered to someone.

Second, *Jesus spent time with him in Q and A.* Jesus could have asked the first question. Instead, Jesus allowed Legion to ask the first question, "What business do we have with each other, Jesus, Son of the Most High God?" (Lk. 8:28). Legion had heard of Jesus and His reputation. He knew that Jesus was a man who did and lived what He said. He had preformed miracles and changed the trajectories of many people's lives. Legion knew he was face to face with someone who could transform his life. His first concern was the possibility of torment. Legion understood he was face to face with the living God and knew he could be toast before taking another breath. Legion had experienced all the torture and torment he could stand. Instead of becoming toast, Legion must have been mystified that Jesus replied with a question: "What is your name?"

Third, *Jesus addressed the very issue that created the hopeless situation of Legion.* Jesus did not run from it as everyone else had. Jesus did not use chains to get control. He went right after it, calling on the power of God to correct the situation. Jesus demonstrated both compassion and action, a combination that has the potential possibility of assisting someone in overcoming a desperate feeling of hopelessness. Compassion alone does not offer the possibility of overcoming hopelessness. Action is required.

Fourth, *Jesus stood firm with Legion following the transformation.* Jesus knew there would be many doubters. When a few people came to see if what they heard was reality, they found Legion sitting at Jesus' feet, the same place he was sitting before his transformation. The community did not initially accept Legion's transformation. However, Jesus understood that helping people through a hopeless situation is not complete until the person is accepted as "hopeful."

Finally, Jesus understood the last step in assisting people in moving from hopeless to hopeful is *they must be willing to share their story.* The Bible says Legion was hoping to follow Jesus. After all, Jesus literally had transformed his life. Not only had Jesus dealt with the hopeless situation, but He also had met Legion's deep spiritual needs. It was time for Legion to walk alone and provide a genuine demonstration of his transformation. Jesus encouraged Legion to go back home and tell his story. People who have had a transformation from hopeless to hopeful have an important story to tell. Jesus knew that, in order to be truly hope-full, the cure was not complete until Legion had the opportunity to assist a hopeless person to become hopeful. In the same way, we must encourage people to share the story of their transformation from "hopeless" to "hopeful."

It is difficult for us to go through a day and not encounter someone who is about ready to give up. Maybe it was the death of a spouse or a child, financial problems, loss of a job, a divorce or separation, a personal health crisis, or one of myriad other crises that impact many of our "neighbors." The step Jesus demonstrated in His encounter with Legion can give us a handle to introduce them to the person who specializes in giving people hope.

Purposelessness: Matthew Called (Mt. 9:9–13)

One of the most evident felt needs today is purposelessness. If we would just take a moment and look at many of the people we come into contact with daily, we can observe many actions demonstrating this felt need.

On your next trip to the bookstore, take a look at all the people heading toward the self-help or the religious sections. (Remember, the "religious" section contains materials on a wide variety of "religions.") Read article after article in your local newspaper, and the personal drive for purpose in life can be found in nearly every inventory. Purposelessness is so prevalent in our culture that it should be considered a highly communicable disease.

As Jesus went on from there, He saw a man called Matthew, sitting in the tax collector's booth; and He said to him, "Follow Me!" And he got up and followed Him. Then it happened that as Jesus was reclining at the table in the house, behold, many tax collectors and sinners came and were dining with Jesus and His disciples. When the Pharisees saw this, they said to His disciples, "Why is your Teacher eating with the tax collectors and sinners?" But when Jesus heard this, He said, "It is not those who are healthy who need a physician, but those who are sick. But go and learn what this means: 'I DESIRE COMPASSION, AND NOT SACRIFICE,' for I did not come to call the righteous, but sinners." (Mt. 9:9–13)

Matthew had been a Jewish tax collector. The position held many benefits, but it also held many issues. For an introvert, being a Jewish tax collector would possibly be a situation one could handle emotionally. It meant, as discussed earlier in the Zaccheus story, few if any close friends. Matthew knew he was not up for consideration for the "most popular resident" in the community.

First, *Jesus helped Matthew to see life as more than collecting money.* Real purpose in life cannot be achieved by a larger bank account. Materialism is not where people find purpose. Having all the latest gadgets and gizmos does not provide an individual with a real purpose for life. Real purpose in life is always about a cause.

Second, *Jesus understood that for a person to discover purpose in life, he or she needs assistance.* An individual wandering aimlessly through life, wondering if coin collecting is as good as life gets, needs someone to invest in them to discover their purpose. Sure, we hear stories from time to time of an individual overcoming purposeless living. However, somewhere along the journey, someone has to support the newly found purpose. Purposeful living cannot be achieved on your own. It takes support, guidance, and encouragement. It cannot be achieved without someone standing in the gap, reminding the person of the reason behind what he or she is doing.

Third, *Jesus supported Matthew's first attempt at purposeful living.* Matthew wanted to share with his tax collecting friends what real purposeful living was like. He knew he would probably fail at street corner preaching. Remember, he was despised by those in the community. Therefore, I imagine he likely began to think, "What do I really do well?" Matthew felt the thing he could do well was to throw a party–inviting Jesus, the disciples, and his tax collecting buddies. Jesus and the disciples had the opportunity to interact with some of Matthew's tax collector friends. However, in this situation, as with so many in Jesus' ministry, the Pharisees showed up, questioning what Jesus was doing hanging around with sinners. It is at this part of the story I believe Matthew's heart sank. "What in the world was I thinking? This sure did not end up like I intended. I threw a party with a purpose, and Jesus gets in hot water."

That is the moment when Jesus provides us with a possible fourth step in helping someone find purposeful living. It is here where I believe Jesus walked up to Matthew and thanked him for hosting the party. Demonstrating purpose was indeed a part of his life. It is at this moment Jesus replied to the Pharisees, "It is not those who are healthy who need a physician, but those who are sick... [F]or I did not come to call the righteous, but sinners" (Mt. 9:12–13). Matthew understood he needed help finding purpose. Jesus was actually telling the Pharisees that He came for people exactly like Matthew. It is hard to imagine how Matthew felt when he heard Jesus' words. Jesus used the situation, Matthew's party, and Matthew himself to illustrate to the Pharisees why the Son of God came to earth.

For Christ-followers today, real purpose in life cannot be achieved until an individual discovers his or her passion and spiritual gifts. It is through the discovery of an individual's passion, and usage of that person's spiritual gifts, that he or she can find real purpose for life. Jesus' words, targeted toward both the Pharisees and Matthew, provide Christ-followers with the real purpose of life.

Emptiness: The Rich Young Ruler (Mt. 19:16–26)

And someone came to Him and said, "Teacher, what good thing shall I do that I may obtain eternal life?" And He said to him, "Why are you asking Me about what is good? There is only One who is good; but if you wish to enter into life, keep the commandments." Then he said to Him, "Which ones?" And Jesus said, "YOU SHALL NOT COMMIT MURDER; YOU SHALL NOT COMMIT ADULTERY; YOU SHALL NOT STEAL; YOU SHALL NOT BEAR FALSE WITNESS; HONOR YOUR FATHER AND MOTHER; and YOU SHALL LOVE YOUR NEIGHBOR AS YOURSELF." The young man said to Him, "All these things I have kept; what am I still lacking?" Jesus said to him,

"If you wish to be complete, go and sell your possessions and give to the poor, and you will have treasure in heaven; and come, follow Me." But when the young man heard this statement, he went away grieving; for he was one who owned much property. And Jesus said to His disciples, "Truly I say to you, it is hard for a rich man to enter the kingdom of heaven.

"Again I say to you, it is easier for a camel to go through the eye of a needle, than for a rich man to enter the kingdom of God." When the disciples heard this, they were very astonished and said, "Then who can be saved?" And looking at them Jesus said to them, "With people this is impossible, but with God all things are possible."

The Rich Young Ruler's encounter with Jesus contains several important principles to help us help others overcome a sense of emptiness. People wrongly assume they can find fulfillment and a rich life through friends, work, a husband or wife, children, activities, money or financial wealth, or involvement in social organizations. Emptiness is a feeling that can so consume people that they can become disconnected from even the very things they feel will fill their emptiness.

Once again, in this story, *Jesus listens to and addresses a question.* Jesus throughout His public ministry loved to field questions. He didn't "sharply" answer them, but He never shied away. The young man's question is about as large a question as a person possibly could ask, "How can I obtain eternal life?" He understood that there was something beyond the last beat of his heart and wanted to know how he might go about achieving it. He addresses Jesus as "Teacher," or "Good Master," showing he had some prior knowledge of Jesus and His teachings. He felt Jesus was as good as anyone to get an answer from for this important question. Therefore, first, to assist people to overcome a sense of emptiness, we must make ourselves available and never question an individual's questions.

Second, *Jesus began assisting the young man with his understanding.* Jesus responded by saying that to obtain eternal life a person must keep the commandments. Jesus was referring basically to the Ten Commandments. The young man knew exactly what he meant. This man was familiar with the commandments on murder, adultery, and stealing, false witness, honor of his father and mother, and love of others. Jesus began the young man's spiritual journey toward eternal life from an understood foundation. Emptiness is overcome by beginning at an understood reference point.

Third, Jesus *took the young man from the reference point to heart issues.*
It is only by considering the heart issues of life that someone can
overcome a sense of emptiness. Doing things out of obligation or
legalism never will result in overcoming emptiness. For the young
man the sense of emptiness could only be overcome by giving away
the things he treated as more important than God. Money and wealth
are only a fraction of the many issues that can be preventing a sense
of fulfillment. For example, it is a mistake to imagine that a spiritual
routine can overcome emptiness. Instead, emptiness can only be
overcome when we place God and others in front of our needs and
desires. John Ortberg writes, "God's great, holy joke about the messiah
complex is this: Every human being who has ever lived has suffered
from it—except one. And He was the Messiah."[7]

As Christ-followers, we must be on the lookout for people
demonstrating a feeling of emptiness. They may be our neighbors,
the person working in the adjoining office, the store clerk, or a parent
of a member of your little league team. They likely have all their
material needs met. But, after careful observation, we see their empty
feeling. By following Jesus' example, we can experience God using
us to bring fullness into their lives.

Fear: Jesus Stills the Sea (Mk. 4:35–41)

How many times each day do you and I do certain things out
of fear? I have to personally admit my heart almost beats out of my
chest because of fear. Growing up in a city that has been destroyed
multiple times from tornados, I only need to hear someone mention
the *possibility* of severe weather and my heart rate increases. Looking
at the current price of gasoline and hearing that it could increase to as
much as $5.00 a gallon makes my heart rate jump. We hear of a new
threat from terrorists, and we immediately begin wondering, "What
if…?" After being paid on the thirtieth of the month, we look at our
bank accounts on the first, and fear overtakes us. Whether we will
admit it or not, each of us reacts out of fear. Those heading toward a
Christ-less eternity around us are regularly crying out in fear.

> On that day, when evening came, He said to them, "Let us
> go over to the other side." Leaving the crowd, they took
> Him along with them in the boat, just as He was; and other
> boats were with Him. And there arose a fierce gale of wind,
> and the waves were breaking over the boat so much that the
> boat was already filling up. Jesus Himself was in the stern,
> asleep on the cushion; and they woke Him and said to Him,

"Teacher, do You not care that we are perishing?" And He got up and rebuked the wind and said to the sea, "Hush, be still." And the wind died down and it became perfectly calm. And He said to them, Why are you afraid? Do you still have no faith?" They became very much afraid and said to one another, "Who then is this, that even the wind and the sea obey Him?" (Mk. 4:35–41)

The disciples were coming unglued. Their hearts were beating out of their chests. Their eyes are almost coming out of their eye sockets. Finally, someone—most likely Peter—actually verbalized what all the disciples were thinking: "We're going to drown!" Frantically, they begin to bail water out of the boat to keep it from sinking faster than it was. Each of the disciples thought, "This is it, we literally are going down with the ship." Then one of the disciples—again, most likely Peter—said, "Why is Jesus in the stern of the boat sleeping? Does He not know we are going to all drown? I thought He knew everything. How could anyone, even Jesus, be sleeping now?" Finally, probably Peter again, could not stand it any longer and held on tightly as he made his way to the stern of the boat. When he got there, he did not awaken Jesus with a soft voice or a gentle tap. Peter grabbed and shook Jesus and screamed, "We are going to drown! Why in the world are you sleeping?" At this moment Jesus demonstrated for us how to help people overcome fear.

All of us should be good at helping people deal with fear. We have had plenty of experience ourselves. Jesus outlines for us once again how we can leverage their fear to introduce them to Jesus.

First, *Jesus recognized their fear.* It was easy for Him to see it in their eyes, hear it in their words, and see it in their actions. Jesus did not yell and scream at them for awakening Him or being fearful. He understood the emotion of fear; after all, He knew His earthly destiny was death on the cross. He understood that fear in itself is a natural human reaction to a situation and is not sinful. The disciples knew their only hope was Jesus. He recognized their fear. His recognition must have initially dispelled some of their fear immediately.

Second, *Jesus sought to understand why they were fearful.* They were with Him just a few hours before when Jesus was performing miracle after miracle. Why was it that they already had done a disconnect between the power of Jesus as displayed on land? Was it because they were now on water? I honestly believe Jesus thought for just a moment, "What can I do to demonstrate my control of the situation and dispel their fear?" He immediately knew that just to brush off their fear would not create a teachable moment later. Therefore, He did not snap at them; He first sought to understand their fear.

Third, through seeking to understand, *He understood that understanding was not enough.* To help His disciples overcome this fearful situation, He had to engage Himself totally in the situation. The players were the disciples, the storm, the waves, and Himself. He could not help them to become fearless disciples unless He was engaged. Jesus not only knew His future on Golgotha, but He knew the disciples would be facing many fearful situations as they sought to establish the New Testament church. Therefore, engagement in this situation was a necessity. One cannot be engaged and only observe and listen. Action is required for there to be true engagement. The Bible says Jesus rose to His feet and told the rain and the sea, "Hush, be still" (Mk. 4:39). In this case, the action was to calm the storm and sea. Sometimes the action we must take is to hold someone, go with someone, help someone change his or her fearful situation, or respond verbally. In every case, action is required. We must see through the facades people create and leverage the connection to bring them to the person who can calm their fears.

Fourth, *Jesus understood He needed to leverage this situation as an incredible teaching moment* that could indeed transform the disciples into fearless New Testament leaders. After calming the storm and the sea, Jesus asked the disciples, "Why are you afraid? Do you still have no faith?"(Mk. 4:40). Jesus knew that calming the storm and the sea this time would not necessarily produce fearless disciples. He had the perfect opportunity to ratchet up their understanding, so He took it. Though He asked two questions, they were really only one. It all had to do with one word, *faith.* Jesus saw that the path to fearless living was faith. Faith is described in Hebrews: "Now faith is the assurance of things hoped for, the conviction of things not seen" (Heb. 11:1). Jesus understood the road the disciples were to travel was going to be tough and hard. Endurance would be a key. Faith produces endurance ("Knowing that the testing of your faith produces endurance" [Jas. 1:3]).

Churches have sought for years ways to connect with people far from God. Understanding how Jesus leveraged the encounter with Zaccheus to address his loneliness, and attempting to model how Jesus demonstrated hope to the demoniac give us the opportunity to bring hope to a person who senses nothing but hopelessness, or experiences only loneliness. We discover how Jesus used a calling to a higher purpose to give a purpose in life to Matthew. Deploying the process Jesus used in attempting to show the rich young ruler how to find fullness can be our tool to use in opening life fully to another person. And, finally, how the Son of God used the frightened disciples can demonstrate to us how we can leverage fear to introduce people to Jesus.

Just because a connection has happened does not mean people are any closer to asking Christ to forgive them and take over leadership of their lives. A process of connecting a person far from God to Christ requires much prayer and reliance upon the Holy Spirit. It also requires that we leverage every opportunity, every open door to assist that person in coming into a relationship with Christ. Here are some suggestions that could help make the process effective.

First, we must remember we lead with grace, not conviction. Conviction is something that is totally in the hands of the Holy Spirit. We do not have biblical authority to convict anyone. We do have a biblical mandate to build on our connections with people far from God by demonstrating God's grace to them and by giving an answer for what we believe.

Second, we must approach the new relationship with "Heaven's Eyes," not our own. "In Heaven's Eyes," written by Phill McHugh reminds us we ourselves are sinners saved by grace: "Only people like you, with feelings like me / And we're amazed at the grace we can find in Heaven's Eyes."[8]

Third, we must see every circumstance as an opportunity for us to leverage the person into a personal relationship with Christ. It may be a new sermon series our pastor is beginning. Or, it may be a special musical or holiday service. Do not forget about encouraging the person to become involved in a support group or attend the Christ-follower's small group, or even going yourself with him or her to a seeker small group.

Most importantly, we must pray. We must ask Christ to direct us. We must ask Christ to give us the words to share. We must listen to and act on the promptings of the Holy Spirit. I am one who thinks God is prompting Christ-followers "like mad"; we are just too dense to hear—or, even worse, we do not want to follow because of the potential cost we may have to pay.

The church also has a responsibility. One of the most helpful things a church can do to assist its members is to become a second party endorsement of the member. A church needs to provide weekly services, events, and programs that support the member in his or her attempts to reach a person for Christ. How helpful is your church in standing in the gap for its members? Are you offering things on an ongoing basis that almost scream to the Christ-follower that this is exactly what you need to take the relationship to the next level? Churches do not reach people for Christ. People reach people for Christ. People look for connection points in the lives of others and leverage those circumstances as opportunities to introduce them to the Savior.

Doug and Sally bought the home next door to Ben and Martha. Ben and Martha were devoted Christ-followers and looked forward to meeting and developing a close friendship with their new neighbors. Ben and Martha welcomed them to the neighborhood and invited them over for dinner. That night at dinner, Ben and Martha learned that Doug had just lost his job. Their new home was a "step up" for them, including a sizable increase in their monthly payment. They were "fearful" of how they were going to make it financially. While preparing dessert, Martha also found out that Sally had played high school softball. That was strategic because Martha was the manager of her daughter's softball team. Martha immediately asked Sally if she would help her coach the team. Sally seemed excited and gladly accepted.

During dessert, Ben and Martha asked if they would like them to pray for their situation. Doug and Sally's response indicated they were not Christ-followers. So Ben and Martha began seeking opportunities to bring them into a personal relationship with Christ.

Ben and Martha mentioned their new neighbors to the members of their small group and asked if anyone was aware of any job openings. The group members indicated that they would keep their ears open and let Ben and Martha know.

Martha and Sally rode to the practices and games together. After only a couple weeks, each considered the other as a good friend. They spent time talking about the softball team over coffee, and they ate several lunches together. Martha all along mentioned spiritual matters, mentioning how they and their small group were praying for Doug to find a job.

Roughly, two weeks later, one of Ben and Martha's group members called one evening indicating there was going to be an opening at his corporation in Doug's field. Ben went immediately next door to give Doug the good news. Doug was very appreciative and applied for the position the next morning.

Two days later Doug knocked on Ben and Martha's door and shared with them the good news–he got the job. Doug could not have been more appreciative. He invited Ben and Martha to dinner on Friday night as a way of saying thank you.

During the dinner, Ben and Martha invited their neighbors to their small group meeting Sunday night, and to their amazement, they accepted. Doug and Sally became members of the small group, and roughly three months later both Doug and Sally asked Christ to be their Forgiver and Leader.

Leveraging our connection points with people far from God and discovering their felt needs provide each of us with the opportunities to lead individuals into personal relationships with Christ. We cannot forget that the connection must be followed by action. We must be familiar with the models Jesus gave us to move people from connection to relationship.

QUESTIONS FOR DISCUSSION

1. Have you connected someone with Christ by leveraging their felt need of loneliness? If so, who? If not, who in your circle of connections is lonely and is in need of a friend?
2. Are you currently leveraging the felt need of hopelessness to develop a connection point into an authentic relationship? If so, who? If not, whom do you know personally who is currently struggling with a sense of hopelessness?
3. How can our small groups be made aware and leverage the felt need of purposelessness? Is there a small group that has recently leveraged purposelessness and could share their story of how this led into a relationship and later into a personal relationship with Christ? If so, when or where can their story be shared?
4. What can you do as a leader to encourage members to leverage the felt need of emptiness to develop a connection point into a relationship? Do you have a personal story? How can that best be shared with your church?
5. How can our church be ready to leverage the felt need of fear? What are the top ten issues in your community most likely to increase an individual's level of fear? How can each of the ten be leveraged?

Notes

[1] Joseph R. Myers, *The Search to Belong* (Grand Rapids: Zondervan, 2003), 73.

[2] Bill Hybels and Mark Mittelburg, *Becoming a Contagious Christian* (Grand Rapids: Zondervan, 1994).

[3] Doug Pagitt and Tony Jones, *An Emergent Manifesto of Hope* (Grand Rapids: Baker Books, 2007), 170.

[4]Michael L. Simpson, *Permission Evangelism* (Colorado Springs: Cook Communication Ministries, 2003), 128.

[5]Ray Oldenburg, *The Great Good Place: Cafes, Coffee Shops, Bookstores, Bars, Hair Salons and Other Hangouts at the Heart of a Community* (New York: Marlowe and Company, 1999), 61–62.

[6]Dallas Providence Homes, PO Box 866903 Plano, TX 75086, or on the Web at www.dallasprovidencehomes.org/index.htm

[7]John Ortberg, *The Life You've Always Wanted* (Grand Rapids: Zondervan, 1997), 118.

[8]Phill McHugh, "In Heaven's Eyes," (River Oaks Music Co., 1985).

7

Community-Based Servant Evangelism I

The Process, Leading The Leader

The process works! Although several books and numerous articles are available on the subject of change for a local church, the following suggested change process is different in several ways. First, the process is proven. We have seen multiple churches use this process to implement successfully CBSE in their local settings. Still other churches have utilized the process to make other course corrections in their church life.

Second, this process is systematic. It takes into consideration the special nuances of local church ministries. Everything in a local church is connected, and a major philosophical change like this will affect every aspect of the church. Therefore, change brought on by incorporating this process must be treated as a systemic change, not as an add-on or plug in.

Third, the process is leadership driven. We are convinced that for any change to be lasting in a local church and eventually part of the church's DNA, it must originate from leadership, be lead by leaders, and evaluated and adjusted by leaders. Everything does rise and fall on leadership–especially when that leadership proposes such foundational changes as suggested here.

Fourth, the proposed process is organic. Though a leader must lead, the leader must allow for a process to mutate and have its own life. Strategic plans with action items and due dates are efficient but not always the most effective format in a nonprofit, volunteer-driven enterprise. Even the suggested steps here must be adjusted according to the church's environment, the response of its members, its leadership capacities, and its own DNA. The key is that the essence of each of the steps be addressed.

Finally, the change process we suggest is modeled in the Bible. Great leaders in the Bible utilized a process to move God's people toward fulfillment of their God-inspired visions. King David made plans to build a palace in Jerusalem and completed it. Only God's redirection through the prophet Nathan prevented his plans to build a temple to house the Ark of the Covenant there. In response to God's call on his life, Paul began implementing his strategy with Jews in the synagogues on his mission to include the "ethnics" in the new covenant of Jesus. When he made little headway with his countrymen, he moved quickly to focus on the ethnics. (See Acts 13:46–47 for this change in tactics.) While neither of the leaders mentioned here wrote out a module for the change process and then followed it, we can look back on their actions as they brought a nonexistent reality into the lives of people and glean from them a process of change management that can serve biblical servant leaders today.

The process used to bring about change highly influences the finished product. Some may be fearful that developing a detailed strategy plan preempts God's hand in the matter. Look at the Bible to see where many of the effective leaders created plans in response to God's call on their lives, executed them, and completed the mission God called them to do. On the other hand, we do acknowledge that each of these spent time in prayer as part of their planning process, and, like Paul's "Macedonian call" (Acts 16:9), they willingly adjusted those plans in response to God's preemptive leadership in their lives.

For example, Nehemiah went to King Artaxerxes with the goal of rebuilding the walls of Jerusalem. This was the first step of his strategy plan that was the result of His desire to honor God with his efforts. He had a plan, adapted the plan to face opposition and fear among the people he led, and accomplished the impossible in only fifty-two days (Neh. 6:15). His plan detailed who would work where, who would protect those constructing the gates, and who would lead each construction team. And Nehemiah was not the only biblical character who deployed a strategy plan.

God had a plan to send His one and only Son to live a life on mission for the Father, train others how to live under the rule of God, die on the cross to fulfill His mission, defeat death in His resurrection, and then rejoin the Father in heaven. Through this divine plan each of us can experience a full and abundant life (Jn. 10:10). It is because of God's plan, which was initiated immediately after Adam and Eve's rebellion against His rule and which was played out in the details of His-story, that we can have the hope of heaven today.

I (Gene) remember once in a heated conversation that resulted from mission-driven changes at Legacy that a deacon said accusingly, "I know what's going on here," as he picked up an eraser board pen. I responded calmly (as I remember it), "So, tell me what's going on here." The deacon wrote on the board as he pronounced the word, "*Agenda.* You have an agenda."

I then insensitively answered, "You're right. I do have an agenda, and I'm glad you finally realized it." Every leader has an agenda, and making CBSE core to who you are and what you do as a church will be your agenda until it is driving your planning and investment of resources.

The Process

As you consider the following suggested steps in adopting and implementing CBSE as the driving philosophy of your ministry, please understand that in a perfect situation these might work exactly as designed. However, a perfect situation is not what you will encounter as you attempt to change your church's philosophy of ministry. Adjustments will need to be made along the way, and any step possibly will need to move up or down in sequence.

We offer this 11–step process that will enable CBSE to become the DNA of your ministry. The first four steps are for the pastor or the key leader in the process. The next two are about the process champion and the leadership team, and the last five describe how to take the process public. Here is an overview of the steps:

STEP 1: Pray and read the Bible
STEP 2. The leadership of the church must own the mission of "Love God and Love Others."
STEP 3: The mission must have total support and involvement from the senior or lead pastor.
STEP 4: Seek to enlist top church influencers.
STEP 5: Enlist a CBSE champion.

STEP 6: Enlist a CBSE leadership team.

STEP 7: Design a plan.

STEP 8: Provide training for all leadership throughout the organization.

STEP 9: Cast the vision to the church.

STEP 10: Implement the plan.

STEP 11: Evaluate all aspects of the CBSE process.

Step 1: Pray and Read the Bible

Philip Yancey reminds us, "The main purpose of prayer is not to make life easier, nor to gain magical powers, but to know God."[1] We (the authors) have the personal experience that too often we did not begin a process of change by building a foundation of prayer or seeking God's Holy Spirit to direct us through His Word. We know how easy it is to start something without taking the time to ask, "Is this really something You want me or Your church to do?" How do you really know that a change in philosophy of ministry to a CBSE model is indeed what God is leading your church to do? Spend time in prayer to know God, not seek God's blessings on your plans. Here are some suggestions on how to make "knowing-God" prayer the foundation of change.

First, it is important that we *spend more time listening than speaking in prayer.* Each of us has petitions we desperately desire God to hear and act on. Each of us has opened up our Bibles looking for answers to key issues we face. God even asks us to bring our petitions to Him, to rely on Him, and trust Him; but to change a philosophy of ministry in a local church to become externally focused is something we *must* hear from God. Allocate time for listening, intentionally listening so you can *hear* God's heart. Listen with your ears and your hearts. Far too often, our desires of the heart push us and drive us to go ahead and attempt things without hearing clearly from God. We must listen.

Consider these suggestions for effective listening:

Clear your mind of all other thoughts. For me (Steve) that is a very difficult process. I first must spend time sharing with God how awesome and wonderful He is. I bring to Him all my intercessory petitions. I also write down all thoughts and ideas regarding all other aspects of my life. If I don't, they will definitely become noisemakers resulting in lack of clarity of hearing from God. Keep a pad and pen next to you as you begin to pray. "Write off" all the "to dos" that come to mind so you can get to them later.

Spend adequate time hearing from God through His Word. It is critical for church leaders to hear God speak to them from His Word. The majority of time in leading the local church, the answers to our questions are in the Bible. However, let us share with you a caution. Every one of us knows that if we want to we can open up the Bible for support for almost anything we would like to do in our churches. After all, we know the Bible better than most of our members. We know the texts to turn to for the "right" answer. Wait and listen for God to speak through prayer. Wait and listen to hear God's direction from His Word. Don't go looking for the verses that support what you think you want to do.

Ask God to speak to you. Christianity isn't complicated. God makes known to His people His desires, but we first must ask. Jesus promised if we will ask, it will be given to us (Mt. 7:7).

Focus your thoughts and love only on Him. God deserves our attention. In our media-drenched culture focus is a lost art. Our minds are trained to race toward other thoughts and images. The most difficult act of worship is to "Be still, and know that [God is] God" (Ps. 46:10, NIV). We would rather race on to the next stop in our string of thoughts or plans we have made than to sit still and listen for the voice of God. King David shared from his prayer experience with God to "delight...in the LORD; / And He will give you the desires of your heart" (Ps. 37:4).

Evaluate what you hear to be sure you have heard correctly. Our minds tend to default their attention onto ourselves. In our prayer, we might have heard what we wanted to hear, not what God desires. We have two approaches to check our listening. First, ask God if we heard right. Meditate on the message from God. Second, return to the Scriptures and determine if His direction is in keeping with His Word. God will never tell us to do something contrary to His Word.

Check out what you believe God is directing you to do by seeking *wise counsel.* The Bible speaks to the importance of seeking wise counsel in the wisdom of Proverbs. Solomon teaches us, "Listen to advice and accept instruction, / and in the end you will be wise" (Prov. 19:20, NIV). "Make plans by seeking *advice*; / if you wage war, obtain guidance" (Prov. 20:18; NIV, emphasis added).

Be brutally honest with them, and ask them to be brutally honest with you. One caution regarding counsel: remember your counselors are not God. We follow God, not those from whom we seek wise counsel. I (Steve) personally like to tell them what I sense God has led me to do one day and then give them a day or two to reflect and pray on the matter before sharing their thoughts on the matter.

Second, we must *set aside adequate amounts of time to hear from God.* The first time I (Steve) heard the number of hours per week Paul

Young Cho spent in prayer, I was amazed. It has been reported he spends nearly half of his day, each and every day, praying. The first question I asked was, "How in the world can the pastor of the largest church in the world possibly spend so much time in prayer each and every day and get all the 'stuff' of ministry done?" The reason Pastor Cho can accomplish everything is because, he only does what God tells him to do, and he knows beyond a doubt this is the direction to lead the church.

For a successful change in philosophy of ministry to take place in your church, much time must be devoted to prayer. Calendars must be adjusted to include adequate time to hear from God. Therefore, some items currently on our PDAs or calendars must be removed. If we are intent on hearing from God, we must spend enough time with God.

Finally, *the pastor and key leaders of the church must understand and incorporate a biblical prayer habit in their lives.* It isn't an hour a day or even two or three hours each day. The Bible says we are to "pray without ceasing" (1 Thess. 5:17). That means as we go about tasks in the day, we are to remain in constant communication with the Father. Jesus taught, "Abide in Me, and I in you. As the branch cannot bear fruit of itself unless it abides in the vine, so neither can you unless you abide in Me" (Jn. 15:4). We must come to understand that the Owner and CEO of the church is with us every moment of every day, and He wants to be involved with not only the big decisions but the little ones as well.

For any church or individual Christ-follower's venture, prayer is always the beginning point, the foundation, and the connection point of the synergistic power of the Holy Spirit using His creation to change the world.

Take a minute to gauge your prayer quotient. On the 1–10 continuum below, place an "X" where you honestly feel your prayer life has developed with the Father.

Prayer Life Scale

MINIMUM	DEVELOPMENT OF MY PRAYER LIFE								MAXIMUM
0	1	2	3	4	5	6	7	8	9	10

Step 2: The Leadership of the Church Must Own the Mission of "Love God and Love Others"

Earlier we touched briefly on the importance of the Great Commandment in the success of a local church's efforts. *Everything* a church or an individual Christ-follower does should be because *we love God* and *love others.* Anything less and our efforts appear to people far from God as inauthentic. If we really do not love God and love others with all our heart, soul, mind, and strength, we are just making a lot of noise like everyone else.

The question, therefore, is, "How do we develop our love relationship with the Father and our neighbors?" Another key question is, "Do we segment the spiritual apart from the secular?" Key leaders must answer these questions. As a servant leader on mission with Christ, you are responsible for equipping those you lead to carry out that mission. A priority in this process is to introduce them to the One who called all of you to join Jesus in the mission field.

We will touch on the "love God" side of the equation, but only briefly because there are far better authors and works available to assist you in developing that love relationship with the Father.[2]

Of course, the first step is to ensure that all key leaders have accepted the work Christ did on the cross and have asked Him to forgive them and take over leadership of their lives. A love relationship with God begins with the knowledge and understanding of our spiritual condition and how essential it is to have a Savior or Rescuer.

The second step is the development of the spiritual disciplines in the life of your leaders. First and foremost in this step is the development of time dedicated to knowing God. Prayer, Bible reading, reflection on God's Word, journaling, and–possibly most important–listening are the foundational building blocks of spiritual development.

The third step is involvement in a local church. Worship, involvement in a small group, and serving according to your spiritual gift and passion are all necessary ingredients of spiritual formation and maturity. The involvement with other Christ-followers holds us accountable and encourages us to "endure to the end." Be careful not to equate leadership or management of programs as "involvement." We want leaders to be involved as salt and light servants to the mission, not managers of our institutional programming.

These steps are nothing new. Likewise, the steps very well might be in a different order according to the process God uses to draw people unto Himself. George Hunter in his work *The Celtic Way of Evangelism* outlines two processes: the old process (presentation-decision-fellowship), and the new process (fellowship-ministry and conversations-belief).[3] Know your leaders as you create intersections for them to know God.

Has your spiritual development process been communicated to your leaders or church as a whole? Do they know how essential each of these parts is to their spiritual development? Far too often, church staffs assume everyone knows this and leave the essential aspects of church life to chance. This is so crucial for the development of the Kingdom that a church must make it core to what it does.

We now move to the critical issue of loving our neighbors. We have hung around churches all our adult lives, and we know how some church members feel about those "outside the church." Those "in" the church often become overly concerned if the person sitting next to them in the service does not dress like them or act like them. Worse yet is the attitude of many church members toward those far less privileged in our communities. Their attitude is not unlike the prevalent opinion in Jesus' day–that sin in the person's life must be the cause for their lack of "success" in life (Jn. 9:1), or the disfavor shown the poor when the *ekklesia* gathered on the first day of the week (Jas. 2:1–9).

It is absolutely crucial that a church and its members genuinely love people if they are ever going to effectively fulfill the Great Commission. We might know how to share our faith, but if our hearts do not beat out of our chests for people who are facing a Christ-less eternity, His Story will not matter to them.

One of the churches currently working the CBSE methodology does not have an issue with putting church funds into community and civic organizations to improve them. Many reading this are first going to ask, "Why are they doing that? Isn't that what our tax money is supposed to do?" However, through the church's eyes, God desires His people to make the world a better place. After all, everything is His anyway. So why not invest Kingdom money and volunteers to make a positive place in the culture better? Michael Frost teaches us, "In a culture yearning for authenticity–the real–the pressure is on us in the Christian community now more than ever to put our time and our money where our mouth is and live what we preach."[4]

How can we assist our members and regular attenders to authentically love people? The first step is to encourage our people to read, reread, and journal on the Great Commandment. Allow God to speak to you through His Word. Roughly two years ago I (Steve) wrote this first step. It made sense to me to laser focus on the Great Commandment. After all, developing my love for my neighbors was one of the most important steps a Christ-follower could undertake. I decided that if I was going to suggest this as an important step, I must have some experience and be able to demonstrate life change because of this daily activity.

For more than two years now, I have read only the Great Commandment in my daily Bible reading. I have listened to the Father point out situation after situation in which I have fallen short in my behavior toward others. Have I "arrived"? Absolutely not. Am I developing my love for others? Yes, I am! Am I looking at more people the way I believe the Father looks at them? Yes. Is my heart beginning to slowly change? Again, my answer is an unequivocal "yes."

Just prior to Christmas one year, I (Steve) approached an intersection. I noticed a man holding a sign that read, "I'm Dreaming of a Cheeseburger." The light turned red and I stopped beside him. I had things to do so I tried my best not to make eye contact with him. After all, mercy scores low on every spiritual gift inventory I take. I faintly heard him singing what I initially thought was "I'm Dreaming of a White Christmas." But as I listened more closely, he had changed the words to "I'm dreaming of a cheeseburger." His creativity so tugged at me that I had to turn around and go back a half a block to a McDonalds. I got him a cheeseburger, large fries, a cherry pie, and a large Coke. I walked across the road to the median where he was still singing and handed him the sack and the drink. His smile grabbed my heart. We spoke only briefly. I shared how his song made me smile and touched my heart. As I was walking away, he asked me why I did that. I shared with him how I had focused on Christ's Great Commandment wanting to develop my love relationship with God and people. He smiled and said, "It's starting to take." I'm now sold.

Second, encourage your people to put their trust in Jesus into practice without sharing a word. Let people see their loving spirit. Serve other people through deeds and not words. Give no explanation for what you are doing. Just silently do for people what Jesus would do for them. You will have to test drive this silent love. In doing so, you may well experience rejection and failure before the opportunity–the right moment–comes for you to give a reason for silently demonstrating love toward your neighbor without recognition or explanation. Teach them "secret service" as taught by Jesus (Mt. 6:1).

Third, capitalize on the opportunities God provides to you to model loving God and loving others. It is just wrong to share the life you call members to without first incorporating the Great Commandment thoroughly into your own life. "Faith without works is dead" (Jas. 2:26b). Not to practice what you preach invites people to question your leadership and integrity.

Fourth, share the things you have learned from God's Word and the Holy Spirit with the staff and key church leaders. You may even strongly insist that they also spend quality time asking God to reveal what they need to do to graft the Great Commandment into their lives.

Fifth, ask your church to spend extended time studying and reflecting on the Great Commandment. Utilize your Sunday school and/or small groups for the delivery method. Ask each small group or Sunday school class, including children, to apply the verse in their lives and to hold them accountable. Additionally, ask them to spend more than one session on this core passage.

Sixth, continue teaching this reality until your people get it. Utilize your personal stories and the stories of others who have recently begun serving their neighbors in love. This kingpin value cannot be taught from the pulpit and demonstrated by acts of love toward others by the pastor alone. It requires that the value already is imported into the DNA of leadership. Unless you can offer concrete evidence that you have authentically incorporated the Great Commandment into your life, how can you expect anyone in your church to catch it? This is one area in which the entire philosophy of ministry will collapse if your church's leadership does not demonstrate love for their neighbors.

Seventh, encourage members to have their small groups hold them personally responsible to live out the Great Commandment. If left to our own, we know self wins. Developing spiritually cannot happen in a vacuum. Each of us needs accountability.

Take a moment to reflect where your love quotient is regarding your love for your neighbor. Do you really love your neighbor? If God were to rate you on your love for your neighbors, where would He place you? Which new "neighbors" have you intentionally built a relationship with as a way of demonstrating incorporation of the Great Commandment into your life?

Love Quotient Scale

LOW LOVE QUOTIENT						HIGH LOVE QUOTIENT				
0	1	2	3	4	5	6	7	8	9	10

Step 3: The Mission Must Have Total Support and Involvement from the Senior or Lead Pastor

If the pastor is not a champion for CBSE, it will fail. Week-to-week members will not commit to any new philosophy, program, process, or event if the pastor does not strongly support the change. Whether or not a pastor wants to accept this reality and responsibility, it remains true that if a change process is to be incorporated throughout the church, his support is of pivotal importance. Pastoral leadership for the change will make or break the proposed change.

Prior to dealing with specifics, it is important for the senior or lead pastor to understand fully that implementing CBSE involves a church culture change. To encourage members to serve in the community as salt and light servants without addressing the church's culture or philosophy of ministry is like committing to lose weight without changing either your diet or lifestyle. We feel a need to be perfectly clear about this. Without a genuine change in your philosophy of ministry/methodology, CBSE will not take hold. It will be nothing but a new program that will quickly become old and can be added to your shelf of "tried thats." We also understand the potential cost of leadership. Heifetz and Linsky got it right when they concluded:

> The deeper the change and the greater the amount of new learning required, the more resistance there will be and, thus, the greater the danger to those who lead. For this reason, people often try to avoid the dangers, either consciously or subconsciously, by treating an adaptive challenge as if it were a technical one. This is why we see so much more routine management than leadership in our society.[5]

We are promoting an "adaptive change" (ministry philosophy), and we know from experience that this can be all-consuming, and, as Heifetz and Linsky warned, quite dangerous to the leader. This is one reason why pastors like business leaders would rather manage than lead.

Because the pastor's buy-in is so crucial, taking time to honestly answer the following questions will allow you to understand your (or your pastor's) likelihood of leading your church into an effective CBSE culture.

Question Scale

Answer each question on a scale: 1 low – 5 high.

1. I understand Community-Based Servant Evangelism is a philosophy of ministry, not a program.

       1   2   3   4   5

2. It excites me to see members serving according to their spiritual gift and passion.

       1   2   3   4   5

3. It excites me to see church members leading people into a personal relationship with Christ.

       1   2   3   4   5

4. I am a permission-giving leader.

    1   2   3   4   5

5. I am an enabling leader.

    1   2   3   4   5

6. I understand change is a process.

    1   2   3   4   5

7. After developing a plan, I have little difficulty in accepting necessary organic adjustments in the implementation stage.

    1   2   3   4   5

8. I see Community-Based Servant Evangelism as a philosophy of ministry that will fit our church for the long haul.

    1   2   3   4   5

9. I understand Community-Based Servant Evangelism as a philosophy of ministry that our church is being directed by God to incorporate into its DNA.

    1   2   3   4   5

10. I enjoy spending time with people far from God as much as I do with church members.

    1   2   3   4   5

11. I am personally willing to serve a local community or civic organization, which will provide me an opportunity to be salt and light with those I come into contact with.

    1   2   3   4   5

12. I enjoy initiating a relationship with someone far from God.

    1   2   3   4   5

If you cannot honestly answer the twelve questions with 4s and 5s, you may consider pausing long enough to get 4s and 5s to those questions. Without a sense of God-given confidence, a philosophy of ministry change can easily cause more problems than solutions.

For a church to commit to CBSE as your way of doing ministry means every key leader must accept responsibility for it. A key component of biblical servant leadership is to "model the mission," not simply preach about it.[6] While you face dangers in doing this, this endeavor has a very positive upside. For a pastor to be connected to God in such a way that he seriously considers making such a major philosophy change has the great possibility of producing a great ride. Every pastor or key leader needs to keep in mind what Ron Martoia observes, "Leadership is about God releasing His outlandish hopes and dreams through a certain personality, in a certain context, for a certain time, with a certain people."[7]

Prior to the pastor sharing the idea with other church staff or key church leaders, he must spend a great deal of time in prayer. The standard should be to "spend as much time in prayer as in planning."[8] With all the other responsibilities that a pastor has, this is difficult. However, to proceed without definitely hearing from God is a mistake and will most likely erode his leadership and wreck both his ministry and the church.

Pastors also must realize that giving the strategy lip service is far from adequate support. The pastor must demonstrate by his leadership, adequate funding, presence, and reiteration how critical the CBSE process is to fulfilling God's vision for the church. He must repeatedly connect the vision of the church with the new philosophy. In short, an effective CBSE process hinges on the support of the local church pastor.

If the pastor desires to move the church toward a CBSE strategy, the vision should first be cast with the church's leadership team, elders, or deacons. Senior leadership of a church capitalizes on the gifts and abilities God has entrusted to the church by involving them in the development of the vision and strategy for a philosophy change. The church's leaders should be kept well aware of the importance and the steps that will be taking place over the coming months. Key leaders of the church can supply prospective leadership for the process. Others can supply needed support from other church members. Neglecting to utilize a church's key leaders will put the new philosophy of ministry at risk.

The pastor must also realize that there will be some up-front cost for implementation of the CBSE model. Unless this evangelism strategy is shared in a church's budget development process, monies will need either to be added or diverted to the philosophy. If adequate funding is not available, the pastor and key church leadership should work the strategy plan at a slower pace. Many great ideas, plans, and strategies never get off the ground due to inadequate funding. In addition, each of the remaining steps has some costs associated with them to bring about completion and implementation.

The Importance of How You Make Decisions

The pastor should realize the importance of how and who makes decisions in the church. "Who decided this?" may be a lingering question among your people as you lead them. Without a clear path for communication and authority, chaos, not progress, can result from change. How do you effectively help others decide to get on the train of CBSE?

Ron Lewis consulted often about this process, and we want to share some of his insights with you. Ron said that the first key ingredient is to listen. The worst thing a leader can do in the decision-making process is to voice his or her opinion before anyone else can. This will always short-change the discussion. When a pastor is excited about a philosophy change and the potential result, he often neglects listening to those he is trying to motivate to join him. Leadership involves as much listening as vision casting in the decision-making process.

Ron stated, "There are two classes of decisions: easy and hard. Using rational, objective data and obvious information can lead to fairly easy conclusions for some decisions."[9] Tom Peters said, "People, including managers, do not live by pie charts alone... People live, reason, and are moved by symbols and stories."[10] However, sometimes statistical data can be part of making an easy decision. For example, when the finance team can demonstrate on a spreadsheet that a church's spending has outpaced its giving, the decision to cut back on what you spend is an easy one. (The hard part is deciding what to stop spending on.) You can come to some fairly obvious decisions based on the facts based on things such as demographics, trends inside and outside the church membership, and physical surroundings.

Ron would continue by saying, "There are 'bet-your-life' decisions for which there are no obvious right or wrong answers and no way to gather objective data."[11] CBSE can be a "bet-your-life" decision that the church as a whole must embrace before you can move forward. How do you come to the point at which you will "bet your life" on what you have trusted God has led you to do? We believe that the source of this realization and confidence to carry out such a mission results from a clear call from God. Confidence comes from the certainty of God's call, not the data from facts and figures. Paul stood against "biblical" data for not including the ethnics in the covenant God made with Israel–because of Christ's call on his life, not because data supported his choices.[12]

You will come to some decisions that you feel you will be betting your life on in the process of decision-making around CBSE. Make sure the spiritual disciplines mentioned above are part of your lifestyle before you try to "out-argue" or debate those opposed to this strategy. Sometimes all you will have is the confidence of the call against a battery of data and opinion.

Finally, as Ron Lewis would advise, "Postpone until you reach a decision that is right for you."[13] Steven Sample, president of the University of Southern California, adds light to this insight, "1. Never make a decision yourself that can reasonably be delegated to a lieutenant. 2. Never make a decision today that can reasonably be put off to tomorrow."[14]

Leadership in All Directions

To make a philosophy change in the church, the pastor should be aware of the enormous task he is facing. To lead through a philosophy or methodology change, the pastor will be called to a higher level of leadership. Dee Hock[15] describes the percentage of time a successful pastor/leader must exercise leadership "down," but also "up," "sideways," and "of self."[16]

Hock found that successful leaders lead "up" 25 percent of the time. That would include leading the board of elders, deacons, or leadership team. This is the team of people to whom you not only have accountability, but also on whom you lean for support, assistance, ideas, and leadership. Casting God-honoring visions, demonstrating in tangible ways your spiritual development, sharing with them your failures, and sharing your joys and successes all are parts of leading upwards. Paul demonstrated this reality over and over, as he worked with the newly formed churches of the New Testament. Paul sought to do whatever it took for the churches in Philippi, Corinth, Ephesus, and all the other locations to prevail.

Second, according to Hock, a successful leader spends 20 percent of his/her time leading "sideways." In a local church, this would be leading your staff. Ask these key questions as you lead "sideways."

- "Am I empowering my staff, or am I micro-managing them?"
- "Is the staff just like me, with the same strengths and weaknesses?"
- "Have I hired individuals that are superior leaders, or do I only consider hiring church staff members that have less leadership ability than I?"
- "Have I adequately communicated what I believe is God's direction and vision for the church? Am I willing to allow them to assist in fine-tuning the vision?"
- "Do the staff find fulfillment in their ministries?"

- "Am I calling them to a higher level of leadership?"
- "How often do they have to come to me to ask permission for ideas or projects they may have?"

To change the philosophy of a church, the pastor must demonstrate a high level of leadership sideways.

Third, Hock found that successful leaders "lead down" only 5 percent of the time. At first, we thought this was an editing error. How could a successful leader lead down only 5 percent of the time? Upon further inspection of our own experience, we found that leading "up" and "sideways" produced so much leadership "down" that we truly spent less time doing that than as commonly accepted.

Successful leaders not only empower their staff to lead, but they also empower *church leaders and members* to lead. We want to caution you against seeing church leaders and members as those "down" or "under" you. We agree with Eugene Peterson's and others' frustration that the distinction between laity and clergy has created a leadership rift that has derailed the church from its potential as the people of God.[17] Successful leaders receive their greatest blessing not by having their great plan come together, but through having volunteers and members successfully accomplishing together something that advances the kingdom. Successful leaders are great listeners and cheerleaders. They want to know how the battle on the front lines is going and what resource allocations are necessary to make the endeavor successful. And, they honestly enjoy thanking people for the contribution they make for the mission of the church. They look for ways not only to honor them but creative ways to thank them.

Finally, Hock observed that the prevailing leader leads his or her self 50 percent of the time. Nehemiah demonstrated this type of leadership in leading the people in the rebuilding of the walls. He effectively led sideways and down. However, if we were to point to one single reason why Nehemiah was so successful as a leader, we would point to the fact that he took seriously his leadership of himself. He refused privileges accorded to most leaders and served alongside those he led. He did what was necessary to lead himself as he expected others to lead (Neh. 5:14–16).

Successful leaders understand the implications of self-leadership in the successful fulfillment of the vision.[18] They are prayed up, read up, and listened up individuals in awe of how the Creator and Sustainer of the universe could possibly use them. They are always looking for ways to improve their leadership and their walk with the Father. They are what we call *Galatians 5:22–23 leaders*: "But the fruit of the Spirit is love, joy, peace, patience, kindness, goodness, faithfulness, gentleness, self-control; against such things there is no law." They demonstrate all the fruits of the Spirit in tangible ways through their leadership of self and others.

Jesus modeled self-leadership for each of us. He understood completely what He was to accomplish. He had a plan and worked it tenaciously. Jesus constantly stayed in touch with the Father, who provided clarity and assurance. He locked His eyes on the goal and never took them off of it. He stayed true to His word and accomplished His mission totally and completely. He could eternally say, "It is finished," as He completed His mission to be the sacrificial "Lamb of God who takes away the sin of the world" (Jn. 1:29).

It is important that the pastor understand how committed he is to a change in the philosophy of ministry. If you are the pastor or key leader, where are you on the continuum listed below? Are you a 10, sold out, no turning back? Or, is your commitment low and uncertain? If you are not the pastor, where do you feel your pastor currently is? A total commitment is an essential building block for changing the philosophy of ministry.

Low Commitment Scale

LOW COMMITMENT										SOLD OUT
0	1	2	3	4	5	6	7	8	9	10

Step 4: Seek to Enlist Top Church Influencers

Most churches have a process of decision-making and church organization outlined in either their church constitution or by-laws. One of the mistakes we see most often in a local church is a pastor who follows the outlined process of making decisions legalistically. Just as the Pharisees had what was referred to as an "Oral Tradition" outside the written tradition of Scripture, local churches have a "church tradition" outside their written, governing documents. Some things work according to the constitution and by-laws, and others do not. An important aspect of leading change in a local church is that the pastor understands which matters need to navigate through the formal process and which do not. One of the outside-the-documents-ways of doing things is through key "influencers" in the church. In matters involving philosophical and methodological change, the pastor or key leader must enlist top church influencers to be effective.

Every church has church members who can make or break anything new or innovative proposed by the elected or appointed leadership. Some are on key teams. Some are elders or deacons, and some are not. To exclude them in your decision-making process is to overlook how your church really operates.

Many of these men and women are often quiet individuals whom you never hear from unless something new is proposed. They often trust and are very supportive of the church leadership and the printed process in the constitution/by-laws, except when the changes impact their perceived way of doing things. These self- or group-recognized influencers expect the pastor to "bounce" these issues off them before anything is actually done.

You might think these are power-hungry individuals holding the church hostage. Why would any member expect the pastor to bypass the outlined process in our church constitution/by-laws? Truthfully, some of the top influencers of any church are individuals who seek individual power. They do enjoy having the pastor come to them before anything can be done. Given this reality, your initial thoughts are that they must be troublemakers. However, in many cases they are not. We see from the saga of the early church's development that Paul was plagued by traditionalists who genuinely believed they defended the ways of God by insisting the ethnics bear the same sign of the covenant every other male had done for centuries as part of their commitment to Jesus as the Messiah.[19]

We have found that most of these individuals love Christ and their church. Their hearts' desire is for their church to fulfill its vision and mission. These individuals have the insight and wisdom to make a good idea great. To deny these individuals input into the process can result in a leadership disaster.

How many influencers will your church have? True church size is generally a determining factor. However, to fall into the trap of thinking, "We are a small church and have only five or six," can be a critical mistake. The bottom line is that some churches have five or six, others have ten to twelve, and others have more than twenty.

Therefore, a change of such proportions as making CBSE your philosophy of ministry must include these individuals. However, you must first identify who they really are. You can locate these individuals in numerous ways. One way is to ask members, "Who influences you?" Another approach to asking this same question is, "Whose thoughts are important for you to know?" A second way to identify them is to observe where members' eyes gravitate when a vote is taken or a leadership decision is made. Third, observe that, when certain people speak, everyone listens. Fourth, find out which members are influential community or civic leaders. They may command leadership within the church, too. Fifth, ask, "Who are the long-term members who have been be faithful to the church through the ministry of several pastors?" And, finally, ask, "Who has led out in the past during a time of philosophical or cultural change, or, who are the experienced or seasoned leaders whom others have followed in the past?

A second issue is regarding to how to get influencers' input and engage them in the mission without unduly empowering them to submarine the project. You may need to address these individuals on a one-on-one basis. Others can be grouped with one or two other individuals. However, in most cases, it is wise for the pastor or key leader to meet with your church's top influencers. This is not something to delegate to another staff member or key church member. Leaders follow leaders, and they will want to test your mettle before they agree to throw their influence behind your leadership.

Finally, for those key influencers who are currently a part of the leadership team—elders, deacons, etc.—you must ask, "Do I meet with them prior to unveiling the concept to the larger leadership group?" The answer to this question lies in the following questions.

- Is this individual someone who requires prior knowledge or not? Your answer will be based on rather or not the person is a positional or natural leader.
- Is this proposed change in an area of their passion or expertise?
- Can the individual provide insight on how to address other top church influencers?
- Can you obtain the individual's best thoughts one-on-one or in a group?
- Are any of the individuals so influential that if they are not on board with the plan it will never fly?

Finally, those with the true gift of leadership may be frustrated by our suggestions to build a base of support among the true influencers in the church. Just the thought of having to go to individuals who are not currently active or serving on a key church team, or as elders or deacons may be nauseating to you. Before we lose you, though, let us remind you of the importance of keeping focused on the goal of this change process: the goal is to bring about the key philosophical or methodological change. What we suggest is not offered to protect yourself or to give you savvy political advice to reign in rogue leaders. No, we address this issue because without seeking their wise council and avid support your chances of change are minimal. Your goal is not to do things by the book (constitution/by-laws). Your goal is to lead a philosophical or methodological change through those who can lead others toward it.

We have begun the process of change to graft CBSE into the DNA of your church by giving you steps to lead the leaders. Now, we must widen the circle of influence to those outside the leadership core, but who are essential to the process.

QUESTIONS FOR DISCUSSION

1. Is your prayer life characterized by petitions, listening, or a balance? Do you read the Bible primarily for information or relationship? What changes do you need to make?
2. Do you and your key church leaders own the Great Commandment? How are you and your church demonstrating the commitment? Or, what steps do you and your church need to take to become a Great Commandment church?
3. Is the pastor totally committed to becoming a Great Commandment church, intentionally developing "salt and light servants"?
4. Who are your church's key influencers? Who might have the type of personal relationship with the influencer who should have the one-on-one conversation?

Notes

[1] Philip Yancey, *Prayer* (Grand Rapids: Zondervan, 2006), 56.

[2] Suggested books: Mark Buchanan, *Your God Is Too Safe* (Sisters, Oreg.: Multnomah, 2001); John Eldredge, *Wild at Heart* (Nashville: Thomas Nelson, 2002) and *Waking the Dead* (Nashville: Thomas Nelson, 2003); Don Everts, *Jesus with Dirty Feet* (Downers Grove, Ill.: InterVarsity Press, 1999); Bill Hybels, *Too Busy Not to Pray* (Downers Grove, Ill.: InterVarsity Press, 1988); Brother Lawrence, *The Practice of the Presence of God* (several editions available); Lee Strobel, *The Case for Christ* (Grand Rapids: Zondervan, 1998) and *The Case for Faith* (Grand Rapids: Zondervan, 2000); Gary Thomas, *Authentic Faith* (Grand Rapids: Zondervan, 2002); Rick Warren, *The Purpose Driven Life* (Grand Rapids: Zondervan, 2002).

[3] George Hunter, *The Celtic Way of Evangelism* (Nashville: Abingdon Press, 2000), 53–54.

[4] Michael Frost, *Exiles* (Peabody, Mass.: Hendrickson Publishers, 2007), 99.

[5] Ronald A. Heifetz and Marty Linsky, *Leadership on the Line* (Boston: Harvard Business School Press, 2002), 14.

[6] C. Gene Wilkes, *Jesus on Leadership* (Wheaton, Ill.: Tyndale House, 1998), 162, 170.

[7] Ron Martoia, *Morph!* (Loveland: Group Publishing, 2003), 38.

[8] Ron S. Lewis, used by permission.

[9] Ibid.

[10] Tom Peters, *Thriving on Chaos* (New York: Harper & Row, 1987), 506.

[11] Ron S. Lewis, used by permission.

[12]See C. Gene Wilkes, "Captured by God's Call," in *Paul on Leadership: Servant Leadership in a Ministry of Transition* (Nashville: LifeWay, 2004), 36–39.

[13]Ron S. Lewis, used by permission.

[14]Steven Sample, *The Contrarian's Guide to Leadership* (San Francisco: Jossey-Bass, 2003), 71–72.

[15]Information in this section attributed to Dee Hock comes from Dee Hock, *Birth of the Chaordic Age* (San Francisco: Berrett-Koehler Publishers, 1999), 67–73.

[16]See Paul's speech to the elders in Ephesus in Acts 20:18–35 for his "leading up" to those he served with.

[17]See Eugene Peterson, "The Laity Myth," in *The Jesus Way* (Grand Rapids: Eerdmans, 2007), 10–13.

[18]Hoch, *Birth of the Chaordic Age,* 67–73.

[19]Wilkes, *Paul on Leadership,* 82–84.

8

Community-Based Servant Evangelism II

The Process, Leading beyond the Leaders

Biblical servant leaders build teams to accomplish the God-sized task God has called them to complete.[1] While getting input from and enlisting influencers in the church to carry out the mission of CBSE, momentum is created when a broad base of people become enthralled by the vision of engaging the community in the name of Christ and then adjust their lives to become part of it. In the previous chapter, we described four of the steps to lead the *leaders* in this process. In this chapter we will suggest ways in which you can involve *others* in the mission to make disciples of all people in the mission field where you are planted.

Step 5: Enlist a Community-Based Servant Evangelism Champion

The process of changing the philosophy of ministry is far too large and important for the pastor to add it to an already full plate. If left solely up to the pastor, it is highly likely that the daily responsibilities of being the pastor will dilute the focus. The pastor has sermons to prepare, hospitals to visit, meetings to attend, staff to supervise, and the frequent crises that demand time. If a well-functioning CBSE process is to come to fruition, it must have a champion in addition to the pastor. We visualize this person as someone who walks into every meeting waving the CBSE flag and rallying the troops to it. The pastor must realize he or she is still ultimately responsible for the process even after enlisting a champion. To ensure that the CBSE process is implemented, the pastor must continue to provide strong leadership. However, the enlistment and support of a "champion for the cause" is essential.

The champion is responsible to provide passionate leadership for the church in the development and implementation of the CBSE process. The champion should address several important issues.

The champion and pastor must develop the overall vision and process of developing salt and light servants of Jesus. Many hours will need to be spent in prayer and in God's Word seeking His direction. Many questions need to be asked and answered:

- How does deploying members into volunteer positions in the community assist people into becoming devoted followers of Christ?
- Can those who are not members be deployed in the church's name into community ministries?
- Can deployment of a person far from God in ministry actually assist that person in crossing the line of trusting Jesus?
- What percentage of members volunteering within the ministries of the church is necessary to provide quality leadership?
- What percentage of members currently are deployed within the ministries of the church, and how many are deployed outside the church in the community?
- How many years will it take to move the church from where it currently is to where you want to be?
- What is the strategy to get you there?

The champion, with the assistance of the pastor, should enlist a team that will assist them in developing the overall strategy to implement the CBSE focus. (See Step 6 below.) Both should make certain that each person enlisted thoroughly understands and agrees. Passion should develop through the leadership team as they begin to make initial plans for the philosophy change.

The team members must be devoted followers of Christ. The champion must also be careful to ensure each person on the team is capable of providing leadership. People having less passion or leadership ability than that of the CBSE champion cannot lead the development of this crucial process. The higher level of leader enlisted to contribute as a member of the leadership team, the greater the level of assistance to the research, development, and implementation process.

To enable the champion to lead this endeavor, the church must be willing to make a substantial investment in his or her leadership. Books and articles can be sources of encouragement and information. Visits to a few churches that are attempting to implement a CBSE model can supply invaluable assistance in developing the champion. Previously arranged one-on-one meetings with the champions from these churches can provide necessary information for launching the philosophy and can also provide a necessary mentoring relationship.

A few of the churches that currently are blazing the trail in some form of CBSE are:

- The Next Level Church, Englewood, Colorado
- Fellowship Bible Church, Little Rock, Arkansas
- Crossroads Bible Church, Flower Mound, Texas
- LifeBridge Christian Church, Longmont, Colorado
- First Baptist Church, Leesburg, Florida
- Vineyard Community Church, Cincinnati, Ohio
- Calvary Bible Evangelical Free Church, Boulder, Colorado
- Mosaic, Los Angeles, California
- The Village Church, Highland Village, Texas

In some churches, a person leading the church in the capacity of the champion must be approved by the church. It is never a good idea for the pastor to step out and lead something that has the potential of changing the DNA of the church without the key leaders and the church embracing the strategy. This is not the time to cast the vision to the entire church. The development of the strategy, seriously considering all the implications, receiving buy-in from all the key leaders and church staff, and enlisting many of the front line leaders should be done prior to the entire church receiving the vision.

At this time the pastor, champion, and the leadership team should begin making preliminary plans, including an initial budget for the research and development aspects of CBSE. The financial cost to the church for this process initially will be the training of the champion and leadership team. It is important to remember that apart from God, the most important asset of the church is its people. Ron Lewis always said:

> The investment in people is more important than any investment we make in any other asset of the church. People today will only align themselves over the long haul with those organizations that will make their presence and contributions meaningful. Today's people will give their best to those

organizations that will train them and help them develop a better quality of life for themselves, their family, and their church.[2]

Before moving on to Step 6, the pastor and champion should spend adequate time evaluating the church's potential impact in the community. Two appendices at the end of this book are provided for you to assess the health of your church. The Member Volunteer Survey and the Church Survey will provide basic information necessary to navigate the road to a becoming a CBSE church.

Here are some questions as you begin the prayerful process of selecting a champion for CBSE. How sold are you regarding your champion? Is he or she God's person for the role? As the pastor, what have you done to ensure this person is God's leader for the philosophy of ministry change?

Weak-Strong Confidence Scale

WEAK CONFIDENCE CHAMPION					STRONG CONFIDENCE CHAMPION					
0	1	2	3	4	5	6	7	8	9	10

Step 6: Enlist a Community-Based Servant Evangelism Leadership Team

Servant leaders in team ministry are the most effective way to lead a church on mission. Enlisting and equipping a leadership team to lead alongside the pastor or key leader is essential to this process. The pastor and champion work together and enlist this team to assist with the philosophical and practical changes. We believe the champion should provide direct leadership for this team.

We agree that, "When recruiting volunteers, one of the best things we can do is give people accurate, practical information about how and when they can get involved."[3] Be honest with those you recruit regarding the time commitment they will have to give to the project, and be honest with the potential team member that the journey will be filled with many challenges. Leaders gladly lay out the cost of leading up front to reduce their loss of leaders when the going gets tough.

Qualifications for the Leadership Team

The first qualification for team membership is that the individual is a Christ-follower. Many people consider themselves to be Christians, without ever asking Christ to be their Forgiver and Leader. Some consider themselves Christian by birth. Others think that because they know they are not a Muslim, Jew, or atheist, they must be a Christ-follower who personifies your church's description of such a person. However, for the CBSE leadership team to be successful in the philosophy change and implementation of the process, they *must* be Christ-followers. They *must* understand and accept God's grace. They *must* be growing spiritually. They *must* be involved in a small group of people. They *must* know their spiritual gifts and passion and be eager to be deployed. Finally, they *must* be giving of their financial resources and their time to the church.

Some churches have used only elders for this leadership team. They are individuals who previously have been screened according to the New Testament qualifications.[4] How a church determines who is and who is not a Christ-follower ultimately rests on the shoulders of the pastor, the champion, and the spiritual leadership of the church.

Second, we recommend the majority of *team members have the spiritual gift of leadership.* The tasks of philosophy change and implementation are monumental. Those with this spiritual gift will have the God-given passion to lead those in their care to accomplish what God has made clear for them to do. Spiritually gifted leaders are not all the same, and they have different abilities. A team full of multiple styles and skills of spiritually gifted leaders is a key component to an effective campaign.

George Barna has identified four different types of leaders needed on an effective team.[5] The first type of leader the team must have is the *directing leader.* A directing leader is a person who sees the big picture and has the ability to cast the vision to the church and has the overwhelming desire to see the vision fulfilled. The second type of leader needed on the team is a *strategic leader.* This person is very detailed and analytical. He or she loves working with numbers and drawing conclusions that are necessary to see the vision accomplished. The third type of leader necessary to serve on the team is a *team-building leader.* This person has the God-given ability to mobilize people to accomplish the vision. Accomplishing the vision without this type of leader on the team is next to impossible. Finally, the team needs an *operational leader* serving the team. His or her unique contribution to the team is the systems and the structures this person builds to accomplish the vision. He or she is the person who keeps close watch on the finances and processes.

The CBSE champion should be the "directing leader" of the team. In addition, we recommend each of the four leader types have an apprentice who works along side him or her in the development of the plan and strategy. These apprentices will serve as the core team's immediate substitute should one of the other members need to step away from the team. The best apprentices are those with the same leadership gifts, style, and passion as their mentors on the team. In a perfect situation, the four apprentices would be individuals who are as or even more passionate about other community service opportunities than the team members alongside whom they serve.

Third, *team members should be people who are passionate about reaching their friends for Christ*–people whose hearts beat fast for those outside relationship with Christ and see themselves as missionaries in the mission field of their lives. Leadership team members should be equipped to lead someone into a personal relationship with Christ and should be actively involved in sharing and demonstrating their faith as salt and light servants. They should be so comfortable in giving a reason for what they believe that it develops organically in conversations they have with people far from God. They understand and live their lives around the belief that "everyone will spend eternity somewhere."

Know that developing the team members may take substantial time and should not be rushed. Your church may not currently have members organically sharing their faith. Rushing ahead and establishing a leadership team with someone who is less than passionate about "letting their light shine" most likely will result in the failure of CBSE in your church.

Because Christ-followers' being involved in mission results in a deepening of their faith, *team members should have a deep passion for seeing Christ-followers developed into salt and light servants of Christ.* Team members must be passionate about seeing people develop spiritually. They also must understand that biblical knowledge does not necessarily equate to spiritual maturity. We share the belief that "Christians grow best when they are serving and giving themselves away to others."[6]

Leadership team members should be committed to their church. As pastors and key leaders approach enlisting volunteers, many times they consider asking people who are not currently involved in the church. They think their "ask" might be the thing to reconnect those folks with the church. We have seen individuals become active members because someone decided to ask them to serve. However, the key leadership team members should not be test cases in which the attempt is made to reconnect noncommitted members to the mission of the church. Once CBSE is implemented, it will afford the noncommitted member many opportunities to reconnect. The leadership team is not, however, the place for the noncommitted.

Leadership team members also should be committed to seeing both the philosophy change and the implementation of CBSE. While no one can guarantee they can finish the race they begin, those on the leadership team must be willing to make this project a priority in their lives for as long as it takes to complete it. They also need to be convinced that this philosophy of ministry holds the possibility of enlarging the numerical size of heaven and of seeing many members developed into salt and light servants active in their community. They should be people who have overcome setbacks by displaying the tenacity needed to complete a given responsibility. The leadership team should not be composed of the weak at heart, but of those who have broken hearts for those far from God and who will do whatever it takes to see them as a brother or sister of Christ.

Finally, *leadership team members should be individuals who have or make the time to give to this important task.* In many cases, leadership team members must resign from other church responsibilities to have adequate time to apply to this task. Overburdening a committed church member does not allow a Christ-follower to develop his or her spiritual gifts and passions. Leadership team members should see involvement as the ministry that God has placed them on planet Earth to complete "for such a time as this."

Additionally, it is important that the pastor and CBSE champion match this high capacity challenge with high-capacity leaders. Rusaw and Swanson state, "We need to create high-capacity challenges for high-capacity people. The challenge for high-capacity people is not to discern how to more effectively ladle soup, but to figure out why there are so many people in line for soup. High-capacity people don't ask, 'How can we raise the money to start five new ministries?' Rather they ask, 'How can we start thirty new ministries without money?'"[7]

Tasks of the Leadership Team

The CBSE leadership team will lead the church through the following tasks:

1. Discern how CBSE can assist Christ-followers into developing into salt and light servants engaged in their community.
2. Assist in the refining of the vision.
3. Develop the strategy to implement CBSE.
4. Assist with defining how implementing the CBSE philosophy will fulfill the Great Commission.
5. Assist with defining how implementing the CBSE philosophy will help members to fulfill the Great Commandment.

Let's look more closely at each of these tasks.

A. Develop Christ-followers into Salt and Light Servants

For a Christ-follower to become a salt and light servant engaged in her community, she must not only complete the processes within the church to equip her to be like Jesus, but she must be engaged in her community network of relationships. For far too long, churches have thought that an individual must be a devoted follower prior to being deployed in service for the Kingdom. Churches have forgotten to utilize individuals' spiritual gifts and passion as a catalyst for spiritual development. Rusaw and Swanson observed, "People need exercise for physical health and service for spiritual health. We learn from the Scriptures but we grow by serving others."[8] For people to understand the Scriptures fully, they must be incorporated into the Christ-followers' lives. "We don't do our people any favors by letting them attend church every week, living with the illusion that they are growing. They may be learning, but they are not growing."[9] Leadership team members must remain focused on the goal of developing Christ-followers who can live as salt and light servants in their communities. This does not happen without deploying the individual in service within her passion empowered by her spiritual gift(s).

B. Assist in Refining of the Vision

The team should be utilized to refine the vision for CBSE. The initial vision comes from the pastor. The champion has his or her input, and this is time for the leadership team to develop the direction the church will take to complete that vision. As the leadership team considers how to implement the vision, it is important to know, "Visions form in the hearts of those who are dissatisfied with the status quo."[10] They may find God's way on the paths of those things that drive them crazy as to why the church is not the church as Christ envisioned it.

If you do not know the power and purpose of vision, here are some first steps to help you and your leadership team to grasp its power. First, many books are available to assist the pastor, champion, and leadership team in refining the vision. George Barna's work *The Power of Vision*[11] is a great primer on the subject. We suggest the church supply books and other materials to assist the leadership team. Books such as *Meeting Needs, Sharing Christ,*[12] *An Unstoppable Force,*[13] *The Externally Focused Church,*[14] and *The Great Good Place: Cafes, Coffee Shops, Bookstores, Bars, Hair Salons and Other Hangouts at the Heart of a Community*[15] are excellent works that challenge and enlighten the vision development process.

As mentioned earlier, a trip to one or more of the churches employing some form of CBSE can also prove invaluable. The goal of the trip is to learn all you can about community-driven evangelism and filter the information through what God specifically has told your church to do and be. The individual uniqueness of each church must be obvious in the vision.

Third, a weekend retreat could assist in jump-starting the vision development. Invite the pastor or champion from one of the churches utilizing some form of the philosophy to speak with the group. Invite your church's champion and the leadership team to spend a day in solitude. Here's a simple plan to follow. A Bible, pen, spiral notebook, sack lunch, and a park or retreat center are all the man-supplied ingredients needed. Begin the day at 9:00 by asking everyone to select an individual spot to set up camp for the day. Each person is to search God's Word and pray, listening for God's voice or nudge in the direction of His purposes for the church related to this strategy. All are to write in their notebooks what God is telling them about their church and the CBSE initiative.

Around 3:00 that afternoon have everyone meet together and share what God told him or her in the time alone with God. It often becomes a "God moment" when individuals share the same thoughts and directions they believe God was giving them. We suggest the spiral notebooks should be collected and kept with notes from other leadership team meetings to catalogue the team's journey with God. As the vision is developed and the philosophy is launched, another day of solitude might be in order to assist the leadership team with the initial roadblocks.

C. Develop an Initial Strategy to Implement CBSE

Vision without plans is only a dream. After the team has rallied around God's specific vision for the church, it must develop strategies to implement that vision. Part of this initial process should be the development of an initial time-line that will guide the process.

Making a list of potential roadblocks to the adoption of the philosophy is possibly the most important thing the leadership team could do at this time in the process. The "Anticipate Problems" module in Action Management's Problem Solving and Decision Making process,[16] or similar tools to anticipate issues that can hinder the implementation of the vision, will be here. Knowledge about where conflict and roadblocks may come from will allow the team to be proactive instead of reactive. Ron Lewis said leaders are people "slightly ahead of the group they are leading toward a desired outcome, but not detached from the group." Leaders can see roadblocks and problems before those they lead because they are far enough out in front to see them. The leadership team must be forward thinking to see roadblocks before those they lead see them and cause panic among the group. Of course, not all problems can be anticipated before they happen. Implementation of vision is a fluid and real-time process that requires both agility among the leaders and intimacy with the Father.

The development of a working budget for the philosophy change is part of this step. Ask, "What is it going to cost for our church to implement the philosophy change?" "Where is the money going to come from?" If the church budget is already tight, funds might not be available initially. Forward thinking from the leadership team can launch the process on a solid financial foundation.

Finally, the team should take an initial look at existing programs and events on the church calendar. Ask this question, "As you expand your externally focused ministries, what will you abandon? You can't continue to do everything."[17] Hard decisions will need to be made about what you keep and what you let go. Therefore, spending time at the beginning of the strategy development process considering what programs and events are not assisting the church in fulfilling the Great Commission or are not helping members to live lives exemplifying of the Great Commandment will add tremendous insight to the leadership team as the detailed strategy is being developed.

D. Consider How Community-Based Servant Evangelism Philosophy Will Fulfill the Great Commission

CBSE is not the cure-all for every one of the church's ills. If a church is more into themselves than God, this philosophy of ministry will not transform the church. But, if a church has a burning desire to see God use it in miraculous ways, this strategy has all the ingredients to stoke that desire into a raging fire. The one thing this philosophy of ministry cannot do is *make* people available to be used by God. Each individual must make that decision.

Churches say they are trying to fulfill the Great Commission. However, when asked to list specific things the church is doing to complete their co-mission with Christ, many churches can only show you the money they have given to mission causes instead of going themselves. Personal involvement in sharing their faith, intentionally developing themselves or others into salt and light servants, has been reduced to involvement in and management of church programs and events. Some churches no longer organize around purpose. We agree with Rusaw and Swanson, "Remember that we organize around purpose, not around program or tactic. Every program that is effective today, no matter how good it is, has a life span. It eventually will lose momentum. We've got to be so in tune with God's purpose that our purpose isn't interrupted when a program runs out of steam."[18] Simply put, some churches have become co-dependent upon programs and events, and that co-dependency prevents them from being responsive to God's leadership among them.

Here is a simple question a church and its leaders can ask to determine if they are church program co-dependent or not. When a guest or a family joins your church, what is your first thought? Is it, "What slot on the organizational chart can they fill?" or is it, "What unique passion and spiritual gifts do they bring to our church?" True, churches do need core programs. However, in many churches, the list of ministries goes on and on. Once a program is started, it seems to hang on forever.

CBSE allows Christ-followers and churches to once again become players in the Great Commission, but without being tethered to or anchored down by yet another church program. The foundation for involvement becomes the individual's passion and spiritual gifts. A person's giftedness and passion may fit within some existing program or ministry, but, if not, the church can support that person to follow God's direction for his or her life. Who knows? The person's passion for ministry may become a bridge of influence into the community over which other church members may follow.

Joe Ader, local missions pastor of The Village Church, stated:

> One day in October 1998 when I was leading Habitat for Humanity in Waco, Texas, has haunted me for years. That day God revealed something to me that shook the foundations of my views on missions forever. We had been preparing for a huge event, the 10-Year Anniversary Celebration of Campus Chapters of Habitat for Humanity. For the event we would have thousands of people from schools around the country in town, the founder of Habitat Millard Fuller would speak, members of national and international media would be there, and to commemorate the event we would finish a Habitat House and hand the keys over to a deserving member of the community. In working on the house one Saturday, a group of Baylor medical students and doctors came out to help. They swung hammers and helped build the house for five

hours that day. I took great pride in the fact that we had these doctors working with us. Then I was hit with this thought: "For five hours today we had doctors swinging hammers when they could have been volunteering their time to use a scalpel and save lives!"

CBSE assists Christ-followers as salt and light servants by connecting them with people far from God in everyday life experiences. We ask with Rusaw and Swanson:

Does this opportunity put us in relationship with those we seek to help or alongside others who are serving? Is this ministry or agency willing to work with us as a faith-based organization? Will this ministry or agency allow us to minister holistically—not just meeting physical needs but spiritual and social needs as well? Do we have people who are ready, willing, and able to develop this ministry? Will this opportunity result in changed lives?[19]

CBSE deals not only with the front half of the Great Commission, but also the back half. As Christ-followers are engaged in the lives of people who are far from God, they become more and more concerned with where their friends will spend eternity. Christ-followers' quiet time becomes more focused, their small group experience becomes more transforming, and the worship experience more celebrative because they are fully engaged in the Great Commission. Reaching always leads to teaching, while the inverse is not a guaranteed outcome.

E. How Community-Based Servant Evangelism Can Fulfill the Great Commandment

We (the authors) were teenagers when people sang, *"What the world needs now, is love, sweet love"*[20] When Jackie DeShannon recorded the song in the 1960s, the world was at war; and peace had become our generation's battle cry. That message has been on the lips of Christ-followers since Jesus walked on planet Earth. What the world still needs is love, sweet love—the sacrificial, cross-centered love of Christ.

When the religious leaders approached Jesus to trap him, they asked Him, "What is the greatest commandment?"

Jesus responded, "The foremost is, 'HEAR, O ISRAEL! THE LORD OUR GOD IS ONE LORD; AND YOU SHALL LOVE THE LORD YOUR GOD WITH ALL YOUR HEART, AND WITH ALL YOUR SOUL, AND WITH ALL YOUR MIND,

AND WITH ALL YOUR STRENGTH.' The second is this, 'YOU SHALL LOVE YOUR NEIGHBOR AS YOURSELF.' There is no other commandment greater than these" (Mk. 12:29–31). Simply put, Christ-followers are to love God and love others. This is the second core value of CBSE.

The Great Commandment motivates churches to provide opportunities for members to connect with God and to connect with people. Since we (the authors) were children, we were taught that if challenged to reduce the gospel message to one word, that word would be "love." Today, if asked the one-word concept to describe the gospel, we would say "relationships." It is impossible to love God fully and totally without previously beginning a personal relationship with Him. In the context of culture's suspicion toward organized religion and "Christians," it is impossible to show people the authentic love of Christ without first developing a relationship with them. CBSE provides Christ-followers the opportunity to connect with people far from God and to develop a relationship with them.

In fact, people far from God need authentic relationships with Christ-followers to see how we handle problems, crises, and joyful experiences. They need to see our faith in action and the difference Christ makes as we navigate through life. As we love our neighbors, our love for God has opportunities to develop, too.

Some churches quote the Great Commandment less often than the Great Commission. However, through living a life that demonstrates a deep and abiding love of God and His Son Jesus and through developing authentic relationships with our neighbors, we have the best shot at fulfilling the Great Commission. The two "Greats" are interconnected, the same way the two halves of the Great Commission are interconnected. "People want more than arguments for faith; they want proof of faith."[21] Christ-followers loving God and loving others is the proof for which those far from God so desperately search.

Train the Community-Based Servant Evangelism Leadership Team

An untrained team is an ineffective team. Every successful team spends more time training than actually playing on the field. Preparation and practice precede success. Training for every member of the CBSE leadership team is critically important. No rock should be left unturned. Too many churches fall into the trap of launching without training. They sense God leading in a certain direction, and they enlist volunteers for the tasks related to that direction. Then, the key leaders sit down, cross their legs, wipe their brows, take a deep breath, and say, "I'm glad that's over." But just because a team is enlisted and a leader is put in charge of the team and the pastor is supportive, this does not necessarily result in a successful team.

One way to train the leadership team is to make arrangements for leaders to visit prospective cooperative ministries and community action groups. The leadership team should know many of the opportunities for volunteerism in the community and should begin building relationships with them. Team members also must understand the partnering organizations' purpose and vision, requirements for volunteers, and any training necessary for people prior to serving as volunteers.

Another equipping process for CBSE is to research current ministries in other area churches. We believe in the larger, capital "C" church. Duplication of ministries may be necessary, although an exact duplication of services would be a waste of Kingdom resources. Discover opportunities for your church members to volunteer in those existing ministries. Some church leaders may feel uneasy about encouraging church members to serve in another church's ministry. Internally focused churches typically are those that have an issue with this. However, community-focused churches understand that those ministries are a part of God's larger, broader work, and those churches look for what God is up to and join Him in what He is blessing rather than doing things and asking God to bless their efforts.[22] Leadership team members should learn everything possible from other ministries, particularly how they train and develop their volunteers.

We have good reasons to learn from effective ministries. One, they are doing exactly what God wants them to do. Two, resources are being provided to the ministry, through adequate funding and trained volunteers. Anyone should be willing to learn from other ministries that are effectively engaged in their mission fields.

Churches involved in some aspect of CBSE should provide access to quality leadership conferences provided by teaching churches. If a church offers a conference that provides training in a particular aspect of CBSE as the leadership team has envisioned, the team members should take full advantage of the opportunity. The team and apprentices should consider attending this training opportunity to rub shoulders with others who are passionate about developing a high-octane, CBSE process.

Commit to Prayer as a Team

Prayer is the one element that, if either included or excluded, has the potential to make or break the effectiveness of this philosophy of ministry. Prayer far too often is an aspect of the Christ-follower's lifestyle that is talked about far more than acted upon. If your church does not have an established prayer ministry, begin one. If it has one, it must be leveraged to encourage the church to pray for the implementation of the CBSE philosophy of ministry. Each Christ-follower needs to be reminded that prayer is communication with God. Also, remember that the pattern of, "He speaks; we listen," is more important than, "We speak; God listens." The CBSE leadership team must set the example in both priority and practice to make prayer the core strategy for the "love God, love others" mission of this philosophy of ministry.

Here are some ways to incorporate prayer into the CBSE implementation process:

1. Preach a sermon series or teach a Bible study series on prayer. Utilize the giants of faith as examples for specifics regarding the importance of prayer in their effectiveness in fulfilling God's vision for their lives.

2. Develop a month-long prayer guide for the church to pray about specific community needs and how God might use the church to meet those needs.

3. If you do not have a prayer room, create one. If you do, list specific community needs and identify possible connection points through which members might become "salt and light."

4. Pray for civic and community services and programs. Pray specifically for the leaders of the organizations and their programs or services.

5. Take the elders/deacons away for a day of solitude to pray specifically for God's direction regarding this possible philosophy of ministry change.

6. Encourage the church to pray for one person far from God, at one o'clock every afternoon, for one minute. The result will be the Holy Spirit moving in the person and the Christ-followers' hearts beating faster for those headed toward a Christ-less eternity.

7. Conduct a day of prayer for the church. Churches have days of prayer for hunger, world missions, etc., but seldom do churches set aside an entire day to pray specifically for themselves, especially for wisdom as a change in philosophy of ministry is taking place.

Step 7: Design a Plan

It is finally time to develop the plan or strategy. Harvard Business School professors Ronald Heifetz and Marty Linsky remind us, "A plan is no more than today's best guess. Tomorrow you discover the unanticipated effects of today's action and adjust to those unexpected events."[23] Make your "best guess" as a leadership team, act upon it, and adjust as circumstances warrant change and/or as God guides you. The plan should include an overall, intentional, and systematic process. Avoid the inherent danger of making this an add-on program instead of an enduring process. This is the time to put feet to the vision. The implementation strategy must include consideration for the uniqueness of your church and the responsibility of successfully deploying followers of Christ as salt and light in the community. Here are some guidelines to begin the planning process.

First, put the final touches on the vision statement. The leadership team must be unanimously sold on the statement that reflects God's vision for the church. Each of the team members must own the vision. They must all be encouraged and see a great future for the church as it engages the community. They are seeing what the church will look like, one, two, three, and five years down the road. They must enjoy the view. Much of this process will happen as the team begins to seek and wrestle with God's vision for the church through CBSE.

The leadership team must also come to a consensus regarding a description of a salt and light servant engaged in the community. What does a follower of Christ as a salt and light servant look like? What characterizes this person? To get a handle on this biblical portrait, the leadership team may be asked to read and reread the New Testament. Ask each member as he or she reads through the gospels, Acts, and letters to make a list of each and every characteristic of a devoted follower of Christ living out the Great Commandment and Great Commission. The team should gather roughly one month after you begin this process and develop the list of characteristics they found in their reading. Sections like the Beatitudes will provide spiritual characteristics of an apprentice of Jesus, while Paul's lists of instructions to the church and family describe the lifestyle of a Christ-follower.

The list should be compiled and edited by the leadership team and then communicated to all church leadership. Additionally, each ministry and church organization should communicate to the spiritual leadership of the church how their ministries assist members in developing the characteristics for those in their care. In short, to define what a church is trying to help people become allows every ministry and event to become more purposeful. Additionally, team members should have a deep desire to see each member, regardless of age, live out the characteristics incorporated into their lives.

You may be asking why this exercise is so important. First, let us remind you that *everything in your church is interconnected.* We are talking about a total church system, not an additional program. CBSE is part of being "missional," as opposed to being "programmatic," as the *ekklesia*. Without a church intentionally focusing on both parts of the Great Commission, reaching and equipping, neither part will be accomplished. Second, it is critical that members understand that CBSE will enable them to develop spiritually. Third, churches flounder with their current results without a target to hit.

We have provided the "Spiritual Maturity Inventory" for your consideration and usage (see appendix 1 online.) What is different about our inventory is that the individual compares his or her spiritual condition with biblical norms for maturity. The inventory is a comprehensive list of verses in the New Testament that describe what a fully devoted follower of Christ is and does. We have arranged the diagnostic questions or verses around the five purposes of the church for easy reflection.

Another key area for the leadership team to consider is what recommendations will be brought to the church's spiritual leadership regarding the future of each current ministry and event as it relates to CBSE. The leadership team should evaluate *every* ministry and event that takes up space on the church calendar or weekly schedule. Nothing should escape the scrutiny of the team. Careful scrutiny of every ministry and event with their leadership should include its effectiveness in fulfilling the vision of the church.

The process of evaluating the church's ministries and events is where tension and conflict will arise. Change is always a point of contention. Many people appreciate and are comfortable with the status quo in their churches. They want the church to be the one bastion in society that does not change. However, change happens whether we like it or not. G. K. Chesterton, the English writer of the early twentieth century, stated:

> Conservatism is based upon the idea that if you leave things alone you leave them as they are. But you do not. If you leave a thing alone, you leave it to a torrent of changes. If you leave a white post alone, it will soon be a black post. If you particularly want it to be white, you must be always painting it again. Briefly, if you want the old white post you must have a new white post.[24]

Passive change is negative change. Passive change occurs when something intentionally is left the same, while the context changes. The context changes and becomes the new "norm." That which was left the same changes in relation to the new context. The result is change, but in a negative sense, a passive sense. Positive change occurs when something is intentionally altered to "move along" into the new context, even though the truth of the altered "something" may have remained the same for the sake of consistency between the old context and the new context.

Change is a process to which the leadership team must devote much time in prayer and development. William Bridges, author of *Transitions: Making Sense of Life's Changes* and *Managing Transitions: Making the Most of Change,* states, "It isn't the changes themselves that the people in these cases resist. It is the losses and endings that they experience and the transition that they are resisting. That is why it does little good to talk about how healthy the outcome of the change will be. Instead, you have to deal directly with the losses and the endings."[25]

The leadership team may seriously consider reading *How to Change Your Church Without Killing It*[26] *Transitioning,*[27] and both of Bridges' works.

Eventually, the leadership team will need to decide which evangelism training and spiritual gift curriculum CBSE will use. It is important that the selected spiritual gift inventory fit within the theology of the church. Some spiritual gift inventories include "sign gifts," which may or may not fit within the church's theology. Other spiritual gift inventories may include gifts that the church leadership does not consider to be spiritual gifts. Because one of the cornerstones of CBSE is a God-inspired passion, if the spiritual gift training material and inventory distract from understanding "passion" rather than helping, other considerations will need to be made. We have come to believe that there is a correlation between churches that provide evangelism training and a reduced number of members engaged in leading people to Christ. To train people to share their faith as a class in a "study course" program alone does not directly result in an increased number of people following Jesus. To be involved with God in telling and living the Good News of Jesus must become organic in the *ekklesia.* We must be able to share what Christ has done and is today doing in our lives. Engaging in evangelism becomes a catalyst for loving God more. The "Spiritual Maturity Inventory" therefore is a tool that can be leveraged to move members into service and evangelism.

Early on, the leadership team should survey the members and regular attenders in an attempt to learn where they currently serve.

The church may have several individuals already serving in the same community ministry, activity, or civic organization and may not be aware of the situation. If that is the case, the CBSE team may support their efforts by connecting the members. The survey also will show the leadership team all the existing connection points at which members could become salt and light servants. Training the members to share their faith and to use people's felt needs as a way to develop authentic relationships are two important missing ingredients that should be added to the mix or preparation. The membership survey also will show the church leadership the potential influence church members have in the community.

Individuals who serve in ministries of the church and not in community or civic organizations will become motivated to explore the possibilities of CBSE. Michael Simpson states, "Many Christians have so removed themselves from the world that not only are they safe from the world's influence but the world is safe from any influence Christ might have through them."[28] Some who fill volunteer positions in the church's ministries may be already passionate or gifted to serve in their current positions. Leave them there. On the other hand, some that are not serving will fill the positions of those who need to resign to be deployed outside the church as salt and light servants.

Having served on six church staffs, I (Steve) fully understand the uncertainty of church staff and church leaders if volunteers are given the "OK" to resign and serve in some other position. But, consider the people who are in positions and are not passionate and gifted for those places of ministry. They actually may be holding back your overall ministry. God understood exactly what He was doing as He assembled your church. Of all the people who have ever lived or will ever live, He chose the individuals that currently compose your church. We believe He knows they are the best folks to accomplish His purposes in your community. This is one of those "trust God" moments.

To mobilize people into community-based ministry, we believe careful consideration must be given to *creating the position of, and enlisting, a Human Resource Coordinator.* This person's major responsibility is to compose a list of all the service opportunities in line with CBSE and the necessary support systems of the church and to outline the process necessary for a person to serve in those ministries. The establishment of this HR office also demonstrates to everyone how important the new philosophy of ministry is to the leaders of the church.

Do not rush to hire someone to fill this position until you are certain no one is being directed by God to fill the position as a volunteer. If someone does not step forward to fill this strategic position, a ministry assistant's responsibility may need to be adjusted to accomplish this task for a brief time. Regardless, if this process is left to chance or up to every individual to navigate on their own, many may never be deployed where God wired them to serve.

Several significant resources could be utilized by the church in determining the church's strategy–for example: *Getting Real,*[29] *Quest for Christ,*[30] and *Meeting Needs, Sharing Christ.*[31] Once again, remember that it is critically important that the philosophy of ministry not be launched without careful consideration and prayer.

Finally, after much prayer and discussion, *the leadership team should establish goals* for the implementation of the CBSE philosophy of ministry. The first goal that the pastor, champion, and leadership team should establish is the target percentage of volunteers serving in church ministries and programs and the percentage goal of those volunteering in the community as salt and light servants. Some churches have established a goal of 20 percent serving within the church and 80 percent outside as salt and light. Others have established the goal of 30 percent inside and 70 percent outside. University Baptist Church, Miami, Florida, has established a goal of moving toward deploying 40 percent of their members into the community as salt and light servants. The bottom line is that this decision must fit your individual church and must reflect its ministry DNA. If the goal is too high, fall out is likely the end result. If the percentage is too low, serving as salt and light servants can result in limiting the impact of the church in the community. In 1983, Kennon Callahan wrote, "A good objective for many local congregations would be to deploy approximately 50 percent of its leaders in mission and outreach in the community and the other 50 percent in the accomplishment of programs within the local church itself."[32] To be a missional church is to have at least this balance of those on mission and those in maintenance of the mission.

The ultimate goal is to have every member, every attender, and every spiritual seeker serving people. It is through service that Christ-followers can apply the many biblical principles and values that they have studied through the years. It is through serving that the attender might come to realize the need to commit to church membership. For spiritual seekers, it is through serving that they might come to realize how much God really loves and cares for them and His desire for them to ask Him to be their Forgiver and Leader. "The church's greatest impact may not stem from asking for great things from a few people, but for many small things from a lot of people."[33]

The leadership team and champion should establish other measurable goals to assist in determining the effectiveness of CBSE.

For example, goals should be established for the leaders who oversee enlistment, training, and deployment. Goals should be established for both the number of leaders needed to be enlisted and the dates by which the enlistment process is to be completed. Goals should be established for the number of members and regular attenders deployed in community and civic organizations. The leadership team should consider establishing goals for each of the first four quarters of the launch year for people deployed in the community as salt and light. Thereafter, yearly goals should be considered, working toward the percentage goal of people involved serving in the community. By working the process in this manner, it makes the attainment of overall goals much more manageable. It makes it far easier for the leadership to address the percentage goal in smaller, achievable segments, rather than facing a daunting, mountain-sized goal.

The champion and leadership team might also consider goals for the number of civic and community agencies that have members and attenders serving in them. When more agencies are being served, potential connection points increase exponentially. With more connection points, the potential numerical size of heaven can increase.

Gene's training manual for servant leaders, *Jesus on Leadership*,[34] contains a spiritual gift inventory in Bible study material on the leadership qualities of Jesus. This training workbook can be adapted for usage by a CBSE philosophy of ministry.

How does an individual know that a particular volunteer position is a match? Kenneth Callahan states that the following characteristics are important factors to consider as one matches a given person with a given leadership responsibility in the life and mission of a congregation.

Specific competencies and skills that match well with the job specifications and objectives that you hope will be accomplished in the particular leadership position:

- General competencies in work patterns.
- Compassion in human relationships.
- Commitment to the specific leadership post.
- Commitment to the church's mission in the world.
- Life strengths in productive situations.
- Life strengths in stress and conflict situations.
- The person's role in prior groups of significant relationships.
- The individual's personal character and self-esteem.[35]

Delivery System

This new method of ministry and church life requires a delivery system. How do you get people moving into the community and find trained leaders who are connected to those people? We are convinced the network of small groups that make up a church's infrastructure is the best way to mobilize people and deliver CBSE to those in need. Small groups develop and grow by serving together. Some group strategies include a season of service together to gel the relationships in the group. If service is a core value in your existing groups, maximize it by simply offering CBSE opportunities for the groups.

Finally, the leadership team, champion, and pastor may consider specific goals regarding how quickly new church members are deployed in civic and community agencies as salt and light servants. A strong indication of the success of CBSE is how quickly you train, equip, and deploy new members as salt and light servants in the community. It is critical to understand that this is a faith venture. It comes as no secret: the churches that live in the faith dimension are those that see the hand of God move most frequently. Erwin McManus observes, "A church begins to live by faith when its people move the things God has clearly said into the non-optional category."[36]Being comfortable as a Christ-follower is not an option.

We can make plans according to how we perceive God leading, but there is a tendency to allow the plan to be the tail that wags the dog. Therefore, as you implement the plan, be alert to two things:

First, always remember that the goal is to fulfill the Great Commandment and the Great Commission, not the plan. Keep the focus on the purpose, not the process.

Second, God is in charge, not the plan. All plans need adjustment. The only plan ever developed that did not need adjustment was the plan God implemented to restore man's broken relationship with Himself.

In conclusion, where are you regarding your leadership team? Are they God's people for the tasks at hand? Take time to reflect on the leadership team by indicating on the continuum below how convinced you are they are not only your team but also God's team.

God's Team Scale

NOT SURE GOD'S TEAM								TEAM IS GOD'S TEAM		
0	1	2	3	4	5	6	7	8	9	10

We are now ready to train the entire congregation to become salt and light servants in their community.

Step 8: Provide Training for All Leadership throughout the Organization

The CBSE leadership team and staff are responsible for training the remaining leadership of the church in the vision, strategies, and goals. This team must create a delicate balance between too little or too much training prior to deploying people into the community. If too much training is provided initially, this has a way of short-circuiting the individual leadership gifts and passions of individuals. The worst move is to micro-manage the philosophy of ministry transition by giving leaders so much information that you stifle their leadership ability. Leaders and volunteers move toward a leadership-training event with more gusto when they find themselves in a situation created by experiencing the vision of CBSE on their own. Therefore, do not provide more training than they want. It is better to deploy people without all the training you know is necessary so they will to come to you desiring help. This may feel counterintuitive to most training processes, but on-the-job, or real-time, training is most effective in this form of ministry.

One of the best possible training opportunities and settings is a retreat setting. The leadership team should provide guidance for the event. A retreat setting allows for a sense of community to develop between all those involved in some aspect of CBSE. A retreat also allows uninterrupted, in-depth training to take place, with times of community building as part of the experience.

The retreat might begin on a Friday evening and conclude on a Saturday or Sunday afternoon. The pastor should share the vision and lead a worship experience. Everything at the retreat must be first rate. The music, planned activities, recreational opportunities, and the training itself must be done in such a way that the event speaks of the importance and high priority of CBSE philosophy of ministry. "Excellence" should be the key word for the event. In particular, the worship experiences should be planned with great tenacity, to ensure a worship experience that the participants will not soon forget. Therefore, the church's worship leader should devote considerable planning and quality leadership to the retreat.

A retreat done in this manner may be a big financial investment. Thus, the timing of a retreat may be scheduled when the finances needed are available. It should be understood that the deployment of more members in service, in their area of passion and using their spiritual gifts, ultimately could save the church substantial financial resources.

Before leaving the topic of training, it is important to understand thoroughly what CBSE can be and mean to a church, if leaders are trained and developed. First, it is important to understand that leaders are not going to show up simply because you cast a vision and put together an excellent retreat. Volunteer leaders commit to something because someone asked and recruited them. *People say yes to people, not plans.* Prayer must permeate this process. One of many issues that can crater this philosophy of ministry is having people in critical leadership positions drop out early in the process. Retention is crucial.

Second, the leadership team must remember how important it is to thank those serving in volunteer positions. As Bill Hybels stated at the 2004 Leadership Summit, "We must become thanking machines."[37] The pastor, champion, and leadership team must hold all leadership volunteers in high regard.

Third, continual training and leadership development is critical for those on the front line of ministry. New ideas, problem solving, and sessions on spiritual and character development should be planned periodically.

Fourth, the organizational chart initially developed must be continually evaluated and tweaked. CBSE is people-centered, so the organization must develop and change with the involvement of more volunteers deployed as salt and light.

Fifth, the leadership team must continually function as enablers of the volunteers. Once the plan is in the implementation stage, it is the leadership team's responsibility to do whatever it takes to equip all volunteers who are serving to be effective. The leadership team, champion, and pastor should listen two to three times more than they speak. "How's it going? Are you being fulfilled through serving? What is it I can do to help you become more successful?" Ron Lewis' words come in handy once again: "Process precedes product. What a church or individual is doing, their strategy will produce the said result. If you want to change the result, you must change the process."[38]

Step 9: Cast the Vision to the Church

Casting the vision of salt and light servants engaged in their community is the first and most crucial step as you "go public" with your plans. Andy Stanley states, "Every great leader, every successful father and mother, anybody who has ever received and followed through successfully with a God-given vision has possessed a form of authority that rests not on position or accomplishment, but on an inner conviction. It is the alignment between a person's convictions and his behavior that makes his life persuasive."[39] Even though this step could be made earlier, waiting to cast the vision until Step 8 is complete allows many additional people to be on board with the vision and strategy. Many church members will have already heard rumors or bits and pieces of the plan and your leaders will be enthusiastically supportive as you cast the vision.

The pastor, champion, and leadership must realize that members, regardless of when they hear the plan initially, will hear everything stated through the filter that this is a new ministry or program. This issue must be kept in the forefront of the minds of the pastor, champion, and leadership team as written and verbal statements are crafted.

How the vision is communicated is critically important. There are many keys to successfully casting a vision. John Maxwell (at the 1996 Willow Creek Leadership Summit) listed twelve keys of successfully casting a vision:

1. *Clarity*–Clarity brings understanding to the vision and the ability to see it clearly.
2. *Connectedness*–Connectedness brings the past, present, and future together. People will not search for the future until they touch the past.
3. *Purpose*–Purpose brings direction to the vision.
4. *Goals*–Goals bring a target to the vision. Goals make the vision real and concrete. They become stepping stones of the vision.
5. *Honesty*–Honesty brings integrity to the vision. When a vision is addressed correctly, honesty brings integrity to the vision and credibility to the vision caster.
6. *Stories*–Stories bring relationships to the vision. They warm up the vision.
7. *Challenge*–A challenge brings stretching to the vision. Nothing of value happens unless there is a challenge.
8. *Passion and Conviction*–They bring fuel to the vision. A vision caster wants to change lives.
9. *Repositioning*–Repositioning brings change to the vision.
10. *Urgency*–Urgency brings intensity.
11. *Modeling*–Modeling brings accountability to the vision.
12. *Strategy*–A strategy brings process to the vision.[40]

Maxwell added, "Here's a key in your asking someone to join up. You must be genuinely sincere in your belief that you want to see him or her grow and be used in wonderful ways by the Holy Spirit! You must be completely authentic in your invitation."[41]

It is important to know that having key leaders on board builds excitement and lays the foundation for the vision to consume the church. The pastor should be the individual who verbally casts the vision to the church. The CBSE champion must be very visible, as well as the leadership team and apprentices. Posters, articles, brochures, and verbal announcements should be part of the communication process for the entire church to understand the critical nature of this endeavor and to commit to their involvement in the process.

It will take months for the church to be consumed by this vision. As with any change, people will be strung out across a wide spectrum of views. In the book *How to Change Your Church Without Killing It,* Alan Nelson and Gene Appel outline the responsiveness to change we can expect from people. [42] According to them, we can expect to find:

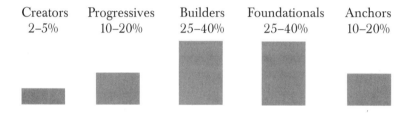

Creators	Progressives	Builders	Foundationals	Anchors
2–5%	10–20%	25–40%	25–40%	10–20%

The *Creators* and *Progressives* sign on quickly and assist the leaders in leading the charge for change. The *Builders* are composed of people who strive to keep organizational form in place. They can be won over by *Progressives* if the *Progressives* take the time to show them how the change will improve the church. The *Foundationals* like to keep things as they are. They believe they are making the future better by holding onto the past. They can be won over with time. The *Anchors* are in love with the past. They enjoy reflecting on the effectiveness of historical principles and values. They seldom, if ever, change.

The importance of this information lies with answering this question: "What categories do most of the members of your church fall into in their responses to the changes you offer them?" If there is a large percentage of *Creators* and *Progressives,* change is much more likely to happen. If there are large numbers of *Foundationals* and *Anchors,* change becomes very difficult. In the vision casting planning process, each of the different types of opinions should be considered. A separate strategy to encourage adoption of the philosophy of ministry for each of the types should be developed and implemented. Every change attempted by church leadership has the possibility of creating conflict and dissension within the body. For the cause of Christ, every attempt should be made to maintain harmony within the fellowship of the church.

As with anything, the timing of casting the vision to the church is important for adoption by the membership. Consideration should be given to the season of the church year related to casting the vision. Because every church is unique, the decision as to timing should be given a great deal of prayer and discussion.

The service or church meeting at which the vision is to be cast should be planned to create a sense of excitement and anticipation. The music, Scripture reading, dramas, and video clips should be used to focus the attention of the congregation toward the pivotal moment of the vision casting. This means that in addition to the pastor, champion, and leadership team, the worship leadership and the arts department must also be involved in the planning of the service. Time is needed for planning, writing, and rehearsals to put together the service. If creative ideas and assistance are needed, the music and arts teams may consult others or a book such as Nancy Beach's *An Hour Every Sunday*.[43]

Consideration must be given to those members and regular attenders who are unable to attend the unveiling of the vision. CDs or utilizing a pod-cast along with a well-crafted brochure should be prepared and placed in the hands of every member and regular attender. It is important to be proactive and place them in their hands, regardless of whether or not they request the information. The leadership team, champion, and pastor should plan an additional meeting for those unable to be present for the vision casting service. This could be a formal or informal time, but must include an opportunity for questions and answers along with the presentation.

Other informal follow-up "Q and A" meetings should be planned. Take advantage of times at which members and regular attenders already are present. Leadership team members and the CBSE champion can host these informal discussions. The more open the leadership is regarding this change in philosophy of ministry, the more open members and attenders will be to consider adopting and owning the vision for themselves.

Finally, what happens in the auditorium immediately after the vision cast is possibly as important as what is said in the presentation. If the pastor, champion, and leadership team members gather around each other to give high-fives, they miss out on an incredibly important moment of vision adoption. Plan a reception or a church fellowship time hosted by the CBSE leadership team. Church leaders must realize that most decisions made by a local church are made in the halls, parking lots, on the phone, and in other informal meetings. Be proactive and create an environment in which conversations between members and team members take place over a cup of coffee or a piece of cake. The opportunity of an informational question and answer fellowship can move forward the adoption of the vision by everyone.

You will face opposition. Moses did. Nehemiah did. Jesus did. Paul did. Every movement of God to mobilize His people to bring His purposes and love to others has faced resistance and opposition. Remember, "People do not resist change, per se. People resist loss."[44] Gene's chapter in *Paul on Leadership* on "Opposition and Conflict"[45] provides helpful insights and tools to maneuver through conflict as a response to the implementation of the vision of CBSE.

Step 10: Implement the Plan

To implement the plan effectively, allow adequate time between casting the vision and the beginning of the actual process. This "lag time" will give people opportunity to respond to the concept, ask questions, and, yes, even produce alternative or opposing plans to yours. However, do not let opposition halt the plans you know God has led you to implement. Set a time to "cross the line" of engagement and stick to it.

Due to people's hectic schedules, we suggest you launch this process at the beginning of a new season of the church year. A "season" could possibly be the fall when school is beginning, or January, with the beginning of a new calendar year. Allow a minimum of three months between the casting of the vision and the launch of the CBSE process. This should provide adequate time to make last-minute adjustments to the plan, obtain key information from church members as to where they are already serving in the community, and to publicize the launch. Incorporating all information pertaining to CBSE in your church's new member class or process is also critical during this period.

The pastor and the CBSE leadership team should be very visible at the launch event. They must be the first people signed up and committed. For instance, if small groups are to be the vehicle the church is utilizing to fulfill the vision, the pastor and team members must be in small groups. They do not have to lead a small group, but they must be regular, involved participants. If serving in the community one Saturday a quarter is a goal, the pastor and team should publicize when they have committed to reach that goal.

Another essential ingredient for implementing the plan is to be on the lookout for the next group of leaders who can join in the leadership of the ministry-based discipleship process. Involvement of new leaders will provide fresh lifeblood for the process, too. Those who join the church because of your new plans to engage the community will bring a new sense of excitement and a deeper appreciation of the results for the process.

Provide ongoing leadership development to maintain a clear focus on the vision and to create a culture of intentionally moving toward excellence. Ongoing training for all leaders is an absolute necessity after implementation begins.

Before you launch the plan, please take a minute to reflect on your plan. Is the plan the best plan you can develop? Where is God in the plan? Is the plan reflective of a reliance on the Father for the success of the plan?

Step 11: Evaluate All Aspects of the CBSE Process

Regardless of how well a plan is put together and launched, adjustments are always necessary. Evaluation is often discussed and planned, but more times than not, we never do it. Even worse, many times the evaluation process is done, but no adjustment or changes are made as a result of the evaluation findings. It is far better never to evaluate the success of a ministry or philosophy of ministry change than to evaluate and not do anything with the findings! To succeed in fulfilling the Great Commandment and the Great Commission, a church must evaluate and follow through with needed adjustments.

First, evaluate the entire public process as you roll it out. Evaluate the vision casting event and follow up of CBSE. This ought to happen shortly after the vision cast service. Ask, "What connected and brought clarity and which aspects of the service need to be adjusted?" The reason this is so important is that you cannot cast a vision once with the thought that the job is done. At a minimum of once a year, the vision must be recast. Some suggest you do this every six weeks. "Vision leaks," is the well-worn adage that reminds every leader that he or she must constantly restate the end picture or people will always retire to painting their own. New members especially need to hear the vision in a crisp, distinct manner. However, it does not stop there.

The leaders, members, and regular attenders of the church need to hear the vision cast often. Nehemiah understood the importance of reminding the people *each month* exactly what they were trying to accomplish. Possibly the group that least needs to hear the vision again is members and regular attenders who have not bought into the new philosophy of ministry. The group that needs most to reconnect their efforts to the vision of the church is its leaders. Leaders get charged up every time clarity is brought to their leadership. Because the church rises or falls with its leaders, the leadership of CBSE owes it to the church to recast the vision *at least* annually.

Second, evaluate the follow-up meetings and the promotional pieces that you developed. Each of these items must be given the "once over" to improve the communication and understanding of the direction of the church. The pastor, champion, and leadership team may consider inviting in advertising and communication specialists to assist with the evaluation process. This would be an excellent opportunity for a member to invest his or her marketplace skills in Kingdom work.

Third, evaluation of the spiritual development of every church member should take place annually. Consider using the Spiritual Maturity Inventory annually to allow members to assess themselves in the five purposes of the church. Use the existing small group structure and the organization to distribute the inventory. Small group leaders can assist in the evaluation using the accountability relationships developed within their small group. CBSE will mature those who participate in it, and that should show up as they assess themselves against the norms of Scripture in the inventory.

Fourth, evaluate the other ministries of the church in light of the church's new focus on CBSE. If the new philosophy of ministry has been incorporated within the DNA of the church, every existing ministry should show marked improvement in reaching and growing people for Christ. You should see that those who now volunteer in ministry are not only passionate about what they do but are now using their spiritual gifts. The leadership team should encourage each ministry, in light of the CBSE focus, to establish measurable goals and to evaluate them at the end of the first year. This also allows the church leadership to stay on top of all ministries to determine their effectiveness and their need to continue in the future.

Fifth, the leadership team along with the pastor, champion, deacons, or elders must evaluate the increased responsibility placed on volunteers to determine which, if any, new paid positions need to be created. This could be done in connection with the budget preparation process, ensuring available funding for new church staff positions.

Sixth, the leadership team, champion, and pastor need to do a self-evaluation of their leadership. Once again, the organization can only grow to the level at which the leadership is capable of providing ongoing leadership. Additional leadership team members may need to be added. Others may need to step aside. Some are great trailblazers, but as the philosophy of ministry has developed their leadership ability is holding back the church. A God-honoring honest evaluation of the top leadership is critical if the church is to continue prevailing.

An evaluation of all training materials and seminars also needs to be made after each training session. Adjustments need to be made in a timely matter to ensure that the process does not become stale. The future of CBSE rests in the training of the individuals before deployment.

Ask each civic and community organizations where members and attenders have been deployed to complete a yearly evaluation. Salt and light servants are to let their light shine before others so that they may see God's servants' good work and *glorify God who is in Heaven,* not give others another reason to turn their backs on God. Ask those served to be brutally honest. "Have the volunteers actually assisted the organization to move forward and accomplish its goals?" "Where have the volunteers let the organization down?" Ask them also for success stories of church volunteers making an impact for the organization. These stories need to be shared with the church on an ongoing basis to keep the members inspired and motivated to be salt and light. Ask for projections of future volunteer needs. This will assist the church to stay on top of community needs. Additionally, it is important for the church to know any changes in the organization that might impact the church, community, and volunteers. If the organization served produces a year-end report, ask it to forward a copy of the report to the CBSE champion.

We know we are stepping way out on a limb here, but consider asking the mayor and city council members to do a yearly evaluation of the church. Ask them the hard question, "Does our church really have a positive impact on the community?" If any negative feedback is received, it should be considered prayerfully. Also, do not forget to inquire about new areas of volunteerism that may be opening in the near future. It is important to remember, if the church is truly connected in the community, the community leaders will be well aware of the church's contribution. Of all the evaluations, the evaluations done by the mayor and city council may be the most enlightening. Remember, the people of Antioch gave the first followers of Jesus the nickname "Christian." His followers did not coin it for themselves, print up bumper stickers, and make jewelry of crosses and fish and call themselves "little Christs." The community observed them and gave them the title. What would your community call you if they chose a name to call those who call themselves Christians?

Kevin and Yvette are musicians who were convinced after their return to the Lord that they were to lead worship in local churches. They had formed a worship band with some of their friends and wanted to tell their stories of God's grace and lead others in worship. The name of their group became "*...from the dust.*" They describe themselves as:

> "...a group of people whom the Lord brought together to help them realize that those that move away from their faith or decide to simply turn their backs on God are in serious trouble. Each member of the band spent years playing the club and bar scene and living the lifestyle that goes along with it. We searched for years trying to find the answer in life that would fill that emptiness in our souls. "You have to understand, the lifestyles we were living with the club scene weren't necessarily our 'sins', but were symptoms of what was going on in our hearts. We were desperately looking for something real, something to satisfy that hunger in our hearts that the world failed to give us," states Kevin. Only when we encountered the love of Jesus Christ and totally surrendered to His will, did we find the answer that we had been searching for all those years.[46]

While they wanted to build the faith of those in local churches, God had other plans. Through an invitation by a relative of one of the band members, they played for the first time in a prison. This experience was foreign to each of them, but they all realized that but by God's grace, each of them could have been among the inmates rather than as a guest with them. The word spread through the Texas prison system about the group, and now their primary ministry of worship is within the fences of state prisons. They call or e-mail after every trip, and we celebrate the number of new people who claim Christ as their Rescuer and Leader as a result of each visit.

Kevin and Yvette have created a connection point for Legacy Church. Fellow members often join them on their trips and support the band with prayer and presence. I (Gene) often follow up a visit by the group and ask the prison chaplain what his needs are to support his work among the inmates. This has led to sending study guides, Bibles, and workbooks to various prisons. We have worked with a family or two who have members in the prisons, and we currently have a plan to provide Bibles for every prison the group visits next year.

The faithfulness of one family has become a bridge for our entire church to reach out to those in prison to share the freedom they can have in Christ Jesus.

You probably are asking, "So what is the bottom line? What would a church look like if they adapted the CBSE philosophy of ministry?"

The Village Church has clearly stated to their members and regular attenders their goal and vision. Joe Ader, local missions pastor for The Village Church, stated their vision is "to move the congregation in this direction by creating online tools that equip the saints for the work of ministry and allow the body of Christ to move in our community with all of its parts working. Essentially, The Village will have 5500+ ministers working in 5500+ individual ministries."[47]

Our Final Thoughts

We hope and pray that our book has been challenging. We know from experience that when we feel we need to improve or find a way to grow our churches we typically look first at other growing churches. Therefore the churches we lead typically make change after change while trying to figure out what will work for us.

Our prayer is *Evangelism Where You Live* has created new thoughts and considerations regarding your church. We are convinced that CBSE isn't about how many programs you have going at your church. Staying focused on *why* God has planted your church where you are must be the determining factor for what you do. Yes, we can learn from other churches' great ideas, but ultimately we must take those ideas and make them our very own. The greatest thrill you can experience is doing well the three or four things God has your church existing to accomplish for Him. May God bless you as you serve your community in the name of Jesus and share the love of Christ so the entire community will trust Him for who He is.

QUESTIONS FOR DISCUSSION

1. Who might be the CBSE champion? What specific steps might need to be taken to develop this person's leadership ability? Is funding available?
2. Have leadership teams been used successfully in the church? If not, what steps might need to be taken to create a positive attitude toward team leadership? Who are your possible team members? Is funding available to train the team?
3. Who in your church are your best plan development individuals? Are they a part of the leadership team? Do they have an adequate amount of time available to volunteer for this project? What unique steps might your strategy plan need to include?
4. Is training of all of your leadership included in the strategy plan? Is funding available?

5. Who or what groups of people do you need to rehearse with in your casting of the vision to the church? What resources might assist you with the vision casting?

6. As the plan is launched, in what areas do you anticipate problems? What steps do you anticipate to go well?

7. Who in your church might assist the CBSE leadership team in the evaluation? What aspects of the evaluation process need to be in place prior to the launching of the plan?

Notes

[1]See how Paul incorporated shared leadership in his mission to the *ethnics* in Week 5 of C. Gene Wilkes, *Paul on Leadership: Servant Leadership in a Ministry of Transition* (Nashville: LifeWay, 2004), 102–23.

[2]Ron S. Lewis, used by permission.

[3]Rick Rusaw and Eric Swanson, *The Externally Focused Church* (Loveland: Group Publishing, 2004), 209.

[4]An excellent reference book on "elders" is Gene Getz, *Elders and Leaders: God's Plan for Leading the Church–a Biblical, Historical, and Cultural Perspective* (Chicago: Moody Publishers, 2003.

[5]George Barna, *Building Effective Lay Leadership Teams* (Ventura: Issachar, 2001), 82–86.

[6]Rusaw and Swanson, *Externally Focused Church,* 26.

[7]Ibid., 209.

[8]Ibid., 76.

[9]Ibid., 88.

[10]Andy Stanley, *Visioneering* (Sisters, Oreg.: Multnomah, 1999), 17.

[11]George Barna, *The Power of Vision* (Ventura, Calif.: Regal, 2003).

[12]Charles Roesel and Donald Atkinson, *Meeting Needs, Sharing Christ* (Nashville: Lifeway, 1995).

[13]Erwin McManus, *An Unstoppable Force: Daring to Become the Church God Had in Mind* (Loveland, Colo.: Group, 2001).

[14]Rick Rusaw and Eric Swanson, *The Externally Focused Church* (Loveland, Colo.: Group, 2004).

[15]Ray Oldenburg, *The Great Good Place: Cafes, Coffee Shops, Bookstores, Bars, Hair Salons and Other Hangouts at the Heart of a Community* (New York: Paragon House, 1989).

[16]Find them at their Web site, www.actionm.com, or at 12201 Merit Drive, Suite 480, Dallas, TX 75251, (972) 386–5611.

[17]Rusaw and Swanson, *Externally Focused Church,* 203.

[18]Ibid.

[19]Ibid., 168.

[20]"What the World Needs Now Is Love," lyrics by Hal David, music by Burt Bacharach (1965).

[21]Ibid.,118.

[22]Henry Blackaby and Claude King, *Experiencing God: Knowing and Doing the Will of God* (Nashville: LifeWay, 1990), 24.

[23]Ronald A. Heifetz and Marty Linsky, *Leadership on the Line* (Boston: Harvard Business School, 2002), 73.

[24]G. K. Chesterton, as quoted in Gary Wills, *Certain Trumpets: The Nature of Leadership* (New York: Simon and Schuster, 1994), 143.

[25]William Bridges, *Managing Transitions: Making the Most of Change* (Reading, Mass: Perseus Books, 1991), 20. His other book noted is *Transitions: Making Sense of Life's Changes* (Reading, Mass.: Addison-Wesley, 1980).

[26]Gene Appel and Alan Nelson, *How to Change Your Church without Killing It* (Nashville: Word, 2000).

[27]Dan Southerland, *Transitioning: Leading Your Church through Change* (Littleton, Colo.: Serendipity House and Cooper City, Fla.: Journey Ministry, 1999).

[28]Michael L. Simpson, *Permission Evangelism* (Colorado Springs: Cook Communication Ministries, 2003), 128.

[29]Ken Baugh and Rich Hurst, *Getting Real: An Interactive Guide to Relational Ministry* (Colorado Springs: NavPress, 2000).

[30]Ken Baugh and Rich Hurst, *The Quest for Christ: Discipling Today's Young Adults* (Loveland, Colo.: Group, 2003).

[31]Roesel and Atkinson, *Meeting Needs, Sharing Christ.*

[32]Kennon L. Callahan, *Twelve Keys to an Effective Church* (San Francisco: Jossey-Bass, 1983), 45–46.

[33]Rusaw and Swanson, *Externally Focused Church,* 206–7.

[34]C. Gene Wilkes, *Jesus on Leadership* (Wheaton, Ill.: Tyndale House, 1998).

[35]Callahan, *Twelve Keys to an Effective Church,* 48.

[36]Erwin Raphael McManus, *An Unstoppable Force* (Loveland: Group Publishing, 2001), 150.

[37]*Leadership Summit 2004,* Session 1 DVD Recording (Willow Creek Association, 2004)

[38]Ron S. Lewis, used by permission.

[39]Andy Stanley, *Visioneering* (Sisters, Oreg.: Multnomah, 1999), 179.

[40]John Maxwell, "Casting a Courageous Vision" (Willow Creek Leadership Summit, South Barrington, Illinois, 1996).

[41]Quoted in Wayne Cordeiro, *Doing Church as a Team* (Honolulu: New Hope Publishing, 1998), 203.

[42]Nelson and Appel, *How to Change Your Church,* 75–80.

[43]Nancy Beach, *An Hour Every Sunday: Creating Moments of Transformation* (Grand Rapids: Zondervan, 2004).

[44]Heifetz and Linsky, *Leadership on the Line,* 11.

[45]Wilkes, *Paul on Leadership,* 80–101.

[46]"...from the dust" Web page, www.fromthedust.com/bio.html.

[47]From the annual church letter filed with the Denton Baptist Association.